HISPANIC HERITAGE
AND PARTICIPATION
on United States Stamps

HISPANIC HERITAGE
AND PARTICIPATION
on United States Stamps

DANIEL T. SANCHEZ

HISPANIC INSTITUTE OF SOCIAL ISSUES
MESA, ARIZONA | 2019

First Edition

Hispanic Heritage and Participation on United States Stamps

Daniel T. Sanchez © 2019

Cover and book design by Yolie Hernandez, HISI © 2019

Stamp cover picture by Tony Baggett (Shutterstock ID: 426664870)

Author picture by Eduardo Barraza, HISI © 2019

Published by the Hispanic Institute of Social Issues

All stamps herein are used with permission granted by the United States Postal Service®
All stamps are © United States Postal Service. All rights reserved.

Q-Productions, Inc., as legitimate co-owners of the copyright for the United States postal stamp of **Selena** (page 62), hereby grants Daniel T. Sanchez the limited and non-exclusive permission to use and reproduce the copyrighted material. This permission shall extend only to the inclusion of the copyrighted material in the book titled: Hispanic Heritage and Participation on United States Stamps.

Cesar Chavez (page 80) stamp used with permission granted by the **Cesar Chavez Foundation:** TM/© 12/9/2015 the Cesar Chavez Foundation www.chavezfoundation.org.

Hispanic Institute of Social Issues (HISI)

PO Box 50553

Mesa, Arizona 85208-0028

(480) 939-9689 | hisi.org | info@hisi.org

1st. ed. pp. xv, 138

ISBN-13: 978-1-936885-26-8

Printed in the United States of America.

1 2 3 4 5 6 7 8 9 10

No part of this book may be used, saved, scanned, or reproduced in any manner whatsoever without the written permission of the author and/or publisher.
All Rights Reserved.

Acknowledgments

It is a pleasure to acknowledge the many people and organizations that provided their guidance, assistance and support in helping me complete this book.

First, I'd like to thank Mona, my wife and soulmate, and my family. They've put up with my stamp collecting since 1975, but they always want to see the new stamps I add to my collection. They each have their favorite stamps from my collection, and they have always been supportive and understanding of my stamp collecting hobby. A special thanks to Mona.

Second, I want to thank all the stamp organizations and stamp clubs for their input and support. I'd like to express my gratitude to Mesa Stamp Club, Phoenix Philatelic Society, and Ebony Society of Philatelic Events and Reflection (ESPER) for their assistance. My sincere thanks to Ruby Hood for her suggestions and valued assistance.

Third, I'd like to thank Jose David Cantu (JD), the co-founder of Trevino TodaMedia and creator of "Hispanic News Online" (HNOnline). JD interviewed me on HNOnline, giving me the opportunity to talk about the use of stamps to discover Hispanic history. Thanks JD.

And lastly, a special thanks to my publisher, Hispanic Institute of Social Issues (HISI), and their founders Yolanda Hernandez and Eduardo Barraza. My first book *39 Years of Blue: A Collection of Life Stories* (2011) was published by HISI's imprint Latino Book Publisher. Thank you both for your guidance and publishing my present book, *Hispanic Heritage and Participation on United States Stamps*.

Contents

Introduction ... xiii
    Memberships ... xv

Explorers ... 1
    Columbus in Sight of Land ... 2
    Landing of Columbus ... 3
    Flagship of Columbus ... 4
    Fleet of Columbus ... 5
    Soliciting Aid from Isabella ... 6
    Columbus Welcomed at Barcelona ... 7
    Columbus Restored to Favor ... 7
    Columbus Presenting Natives ... 8
    Columbus Announcing his Discovery ... 8
    Columbus at La Rábida ... 9
    Recall of Columbus ... 9
    Isabella Pledging Her Jewels ... 10
    Columbus in Chains ... 10
    Columbus Describing Third Voyage ... 11
    Isabella and Columbus ... 12
    Columbus ... 13
    Columbus Souvenir Sheets ... 13
    Vasco Núñez de Balboa ... 17
    Coronado Expedition ... 17
    Juan Ponce de León ... 18
    Juan Rodríguez Cabrillo ... 19
    Spanish Settlement ... 20
    World Columbian Stamp Expo '92 ... 20

Military ... 21

- Medal of Honor ... 22
- Civil War ... 23
- Recipient Branch Birth ... 23
- Boxer Rebellion ... 23
- World Wars ... 23
- World War I ... 23
- World War II ... 23
- Wars ... 24
- Korea ... 24
- Vietnam ... 24
- Afghanistan ... 25
- David G. Farragut ... 26
- Farragut & Porter ... 27
- General Bernardo de Gálvez ... 27
- Civil War ... 28
- Rough Riders ... 30
- Buffalo Soldiers ... 31
- Battleship Maine ... 32
- World War I ... 33
- World War II ... 34
- Classic American Aircraft P-51 Mustang ... 36
- Korean War ... 37
- Vietnam ... 38
- Women in the Armed Services ... 40
- Hometowns Honor Their Returning Veterans, 1945 ... 41
- POW-MIA ... 42
- Women in Military Service ... 44
- Honoring Those Who Served: Desert Storm, Desert Shield ... 45
- Gulf War ... 45
- Hostages Come Home ... 46

Events ... 47

- Panama Canal ... 48
- Golden Gate Bridge - San Francisco ... 49
- Pan American Union ... 49

Pony Express ... 50
Corregidor, Manila Bay ... 51
Gadsden Purchase ... 51
Carreta ... 52
Carmel Mission ... 53

Music, Dance, Theater and Movies ... 55

John Philip Sousa ... 57
Desi Arnaz ... 57
Let's Dance Merengue ... 58
Let's Dance Salsa ... 59
Let's Dance Cha-Cha-Cha ... 59
Let's Dance Mambo ... 60
Carmen Miranda ... 61
Selena ... 62
Carlos Gardel ... 63
Tito Puente ... 63
Celia Cruz ... 64
Ritchie Valens ... 64
Latin Jazz ... 65
Lydia Mendoza ... 66
José Limón ... 67
Lynda Jean Córdova Carter - *Wonder Woman* ... 67
Actors ... 68

Humanities ... 69

John James Audubon ... 70
Palace of Governors ... 71
Mexican Independence ... 72
International Red Cross Flag and Cuban Refugees ... 73
Alliance for Progress ... 73
International Year of the Child ... 74
Hispanic Americans – A Proud Heritage ... 75
Columbian Doll ... 76
Padre Félix Varela – Social Reformer ... 76
Desegregating Public Schools ... 77
Cinco de Mayo ... 78

Frida Kahlo ... 79
Cesar E. Chavez ... 80
Jaime Escalante ... 81
Ruben Salazar ... 81
Mendez v. Westminster ... 82
Severo Ochoa An American Scientist ... 83
Felipe Rojas-Lombardi ... 83
Father Junípero Serra ... 84
Space Achievements ... 85

States ... 87

ARIZONA ... 87
Arizona Statehood ... 88
San Xavier del Bac Mission ... 89
USS Arizona Memorial ... 90

CALIFORNIA "CALIFIA" ... 91
Yosemite National Park El Capitán ... 92
Carmel Mission Belfry ... 92
Alta California ... 93
California Pacific International Exposition ... 93

COLORADO ... 94
Mesa Verde, Colorado ... 95
Colorado Capitol and Mount Holy Cross ... 96

FLORIDA ... 97
La Florida ... 98
Florida Statehood ... 99
Settlement of Florida ... 99

MONTANA ... 100
"Treasure State" ... 100

NEVADA ... 101
Battle Born State ... 102

NEW MEXICO ... 103
New Mexico, Land of Enchantment ... 104
Rio Grande Blankets ... 105

TEXAS ... 106
"Lone Star State" ... 107
The Alamo ... 108
HemisFair '68 ... 109

Political ... 111
Dennis Chavez ... 112
Simón Bolívar ... 113
José de San Martín ... 114

Puerto Rico ... 115
La Fortaleza, Puerto Rico ... 116
Puerto Rico Election ... 116
San Juan, Puerto Rico ... 117
La Cueva del Indio ... 117
José Ferrer ... 118
Julia de Burgos ... 119

Sports ... 121
Baseball ... 121
Golf ... 123
Tennis ... 124

Hispanic Artists for United States Stamps ... 127
Tropical Fruit ... 128
Garden of Love ... 129
Martín Ramírez ... 130
Forever Hearts ... 131
Summer Harvest ... 132
Quilled Paper Heart ... 132
Delicioso ... 133
National Museum of African American History and Culture ... 135
Uncle Sam's Hat ... 135

Introduction

In many ways, historians have failed to acknowledge Hispanic men and women and their contributions to America's history in the United States. This is partly because our identity as Hispanics has been overlooked. However, American Hispanics have been a big influence in the development of the United States since the discovery of America, and many have left their footprints for others to follow. Even before Plymouth Rock in 1620, and while the pilgrims were struggling to maintain their colonies in the North, Spanish towns were growing in the same area and along the Eastern and Southern Coasts.

Many historical figures, events and contributions to U.S. history by Hispanics have been depicted on United States stamps. I have seen and read many books on U.S. stamps, but I have never seen a book featuring Hispanics on U.S. stamps.

I feel that our present youth and future generations should learn about Hispanic contributions that helped make our nation what it is today. I have tried to do this with my own collection of stamps about Hispanics. I have written this book to inform stamp collectors and non-stamp collectors, about the rich and beautiful history, culture, arts, entertainment, sports and other contributions of Hispanics to U.S. culture that have been depicted on U.S. stamps.

When the word Hispanic is used, we are not talking about one nationality or one culture, but about a great diversity of people from Spain, North America, Central America and South America of different race and color. They can be of European, Native American, or African descent, and with cultural ties to Mexico and other Latin American countries and even the Caribbean.

Among some examples of Hispanic participation in U.S. history we find Lucas Vázquez de Ayllón, a Spanish explorer, who 81 years before Jamestown in Virginia, founded a small colony near present-day Georgetown, South Carolina, in 1526. Ayllón landed on the coastline of Georgia and called a short-lived settlement San Miguel de Guadalupe, which was located either along the Savannah River or Georgia's Sapelo Island, depending on the source. General Bernardo de Gálvez aided the American Thirteen Colonies; a city was named after him (Galveston, Texas). The first U.S. stamp to honor a Hispanic American depicted David Farragut on a one-dollar stamp issued in 1902. Farragut assisted President Abraham Lincoln in the Civil War, and was also the first Navy Admiral of the United States Navy.

Each stamp honoring Hispanics has a story to tell. Therefore, in this book I have given a brief history or background showing how that event, musician, artist, or other historical figure portrayed Hispanic culture. Included in most stories there is a picture of the stamp, which will make it easy to identify and purchase from a stamp dealer for those wanting to buy it.

I hope others will want to see, read about and begin collecting stamps, not just of Hispanics but all Americans. Stamp collecting is the world's most popular hobby, and in the U.S. it is the second most popular hobby. There are no limits to the hobby of collecting stamps. Once you get started there is no end to the many varied and interesting subjects you can collect in stamps. It is a wonderful hobby to enjoy, and for me it has been a very satisfying pastime.

I began collecting stamps in 1975 while stationed overseas at Torrejón Air Base, Spain, and since then I have never stopped collecting. I was in the United States Air Force for 20 years, with 14 years overseas; a tour in Vietnam assigned to MAC-V (Military Advisor Command-Vietnam), and retired as MSgt (Master Sergeant) in 1988. In my first book, *39 Years of Blue: A Collection of Life Stories. From a Cub Scout to Master Sergeant in the Air Force*, I write about my experiences in a blue uniform of the United States.

Memberships

Mesa Stamp Club, Arizona

Phoenix Philatelic Society, Arizona

APS (American Philatelic Society)

ESPER (Ebony Society of Philatelic Events and Reflection)

VFW (Veterans of Foreign Wars) Post 9981, Anchorage, Alaska

Tony F. Soza-Ray Martinez American Legion Post 41, Phoenix, Arizona

AACHE (Arizona Association for Chicanos for Higher Education)

Explorers

The early Spanish explorers who crossed the Atlantic Ocean (*The Dark Sea*) were in search of new land, cultures and people that they had never seen. These explorers wanted to expand their knowledge of the New World and new empire for Spain. In their search they discovered a new way of life that explorers had never seen before. The New World was claimed by Spain, which included South America, Central America and North America. The first to discover the Americas was Christopher Columbus in 1492, and many Hispanic explorers after Columbus crossed from the East Coast to the West Coast by sea and overland giving Spanish names to eight states and over 2,000 cities across America. The first European colony was not Jamestown, Virginia in 1607, but San Miguel de Gualdape, established in 1526 at near present-day Georgia's Sapelo Island or the Savannah River, which forms most of the border between the states of South Carolina and Georgia.

Columbus in Sight of Land

Christopher Columbus, the Italian explorer, navigator, and colonizer, made one of the most important voyages in history in finding the Americas, the *New World*. During the day, Columbus and his sailors saw birds in the sky they all knew land was near and everyone was watching to spot land. In time, Columbus and his sailors saw many flocks of birds flying towards the southwest. At that time, Columbus changed his route to the direction of the flying birds. The sighting of the New World occurred in the early morning, at about 2:00 in the morning on October 12, 1492, by a sailor named Rodrigo de Triana, who was also known as Juan Rodríguez Bermejo. He was aboard the ship *La Pinta* and while on night watch, he saw the fire from a far distance and shouted *"Tierra, tierra,"* (land, land). The King and Queen of Spain had offered a reward for the first person to spot land. Columbus claimed *he* spotted the lights of the fires on the island from his ship, the *Santa María*, and kept the reward.

Stamp issued in 1893

Landing of Columbus

Columbus and all the sailors waited for daylight to come ashore and set foot on the New World. Columbus named the new land San Salvador. It is in what is now called the Bahamas, but the natives called their land Guanahani. As they came ashore, all the sailors kneeled down on the sand and gave thanks to God for their safe voyage. They saw the natives and in a short period of time began exchanging gifts with them. This was the first time the natives ever saw men and big ships from a different land, and greeted them as friends. The natives, Lucayan and Taíno, were very peaceful, friendly and helpful to Columbus and his crew.

Originally, Columbus was searching for a sea route to Asia, but landed in the New World by accident. He is still regarded as a great discoverer. As he reached the shore he claimed the land for the King and Queen of Spain. His three ships were *La Niña*, *La Pinta* and *La Santa María*. So sure of himself that he was in India, he named the local natives *Indios* (Indians).

Stamp issued in 1893

Stamp issued in 1992

Stamp issued in 1993

Flagship of Columbus

The Flagship of Columbus' first voyage to the New World was the *Santa María de la Inmaculada Concepción* (The Holy Mary of the Immaculate Conception), a cargo ship called "Nao," which was the largest of the three ships. The *Santa María* was built in the town of Castro Urdiales, Cantabria, Spain. The *Santa María* was also known as *Marigalante* or "Gallant Maria." The flagship ran aground because the sailor who was steering the ship kept falling asleep. The cabin boy noticed, so he began steering the ship. The cabin boy was the one steering the ship when it ran aground on Christmas Day on *La Isla Española*, "The Spanish Island," or *Hispaniola* (Haiti), and it never returned to Spain. The *Santa María* was disassembled and used to build a fortress called *La Navidad*. This was the first Spanish settlement in the New World. Columbus sailed on, leaving 40 men and supplies at *La Navidad*.

Stamp issued in 1893

Fleet of Columbus

The three ships of Columbus' fleet were the *Santa María*, the *Niña* and the *Pinta*.

Stamp issued in 1893

The *Santa María*, nicknamed *La Gallega*, was the slowest of the three ships because of its size. It was about 100 tons in weight and 80 feet in length. The *Santa María* was also the flagship. It had 52 men aboard. It ran aground near *Hispaniola* and never returned to sea.

The *Niña*, known as the "The Girl," was also called *Santa Clara*. It was captained by Vicente Yáñez Pinzón, and was the favorite of the three ships. The *Niña* was about 60 tons in weight and 50 feet in length.

Stamped issued in 1992

The *Pinta*, also known as "The Look," or "The Spotted One," was captained by Martín Alonso Pinzón, Vicente's brother. The *Pinta* was the fastest of the three ships because of its size, about 60-70 tons in weight and 56 feet in length. It was aboard the *Pinta* that Rodrigo de Triana first spotted land.

Soliciting Aid from Isabella

Columbus waited many years to meet with Queen Isabella of Spain to discuss the funds, ships, and crew for his voyage in hopes of locating a sea route to Asia, but there was a war with the Moors in Granada at that time, and his request was rejected. Columbus postponed his request until after the war. With the war in Granada, Columbus requested funds from King Henry of Portugal, but his request was also rejected. Queen Isabella was very interested in strengthening Spain by exploring other lands. After the war, the Queen and King of Spain agreed to finance the expedition, and Columbus was granted funds for the three ships, the *Niña*, *Pinta* and the *Santa María*, and a crew of ninety sailors.

Stamp issued in 1893

Stamped issued in 1992

Columbus Welcomed at Barcelona

Stamp issued in 1893

As Columbus returned to Barcelona, Spain with his news of the New World, the Queen and King welcomed him as he rode on horseback through the streets of Barcelona. The people welcomed him at the gates of the city. With Columbus were his sailors and seven or eight natives in their native dress. They had gold, plants, cloth, ornaments, and many other items from the native's homeland. All honors and titles that the Queen and King promised were given to Columbus, and the rewards that were promised for *sighting* the New World were also given to him. The news of Columbus landing in the New World spread quickly across Spain and throughout Europe, making him a hero.

Columbus Restored to Favor

Stamp issued in 1893

After Columbus' third voyage, he was returned to Spain in chains for rumors of mistreatment of his sailors and the natives. Columbus' treatment of the natives and sailors were rumors by Francisco de Bobadilla. After the investigation, the courts of Spain cleared Columbus. The explorer was vindicated and released by the King and Queen of Spain. Once he was released, Columbus planned his fourth journey to the New World, still hoping to locate a sea route to the Orient. He never found it.

Columbus Presenting Natives

Stamp issued in 1893

Columbus wanted to prove to Spain and Europe, that he had reached the New World by bringing back natives from a different land. Of the seven or eight natives only six made the trip back to Spain, since one died at sea. When Columbus presented the natives to the King and Queen of Spain, the natives were half dressed in their native clothing. Columbus brought the natives by force from San Salvador, and was accused of mistreating them. He was later recalled from his third voyage to explain those accusations.

In Spain the natives were baptized with the King and Queen as Godparents and given Christian names, and were set free to return to their homeland.

Columbus Announcing his Discovery

Stamp issued in 1893

On Columbus' return trip back to Spain while aboard the *Niña* on February 15, 1493, he wrote to Luis de Santángel about his discovery of the New World and the Islands he landed on. He gave a description of the Native Arawak, which he called *Indios* (Indians), who welcomed Columbus and his crew with kindness and gifts. The news about the discovery of the New World, and the loss of the flagship the *Santa María* that ran aground, spread across Spain and Europe. In his letter he also urged the Catholic Monarchs to sponsor another expedition to the New World, and promised that he would return with riches.

Columbus at La Rábida

La Rábida, a monastery in Lisbon, Portugal, was known as the Franciscan *Monasterio de Santa María de La Rábida*. It is where Columbus stayed while waiting for financial news from the King and Queen of Spain. The Monastery was built in 1412 and was a Moorish stronghold. *Rábida* is an Arabic word meaning *fortress*. La Rábida was damaged in 1755 by an earthquake; it was restored in 1835, and declared a national monument. On the grounds is a botanical garden of exotic plants and inside are the details of the discovery of the New World and of Columbus' life and adventures.

Stamp issued in 1893

Recall of Columbus

The King and Queen recalled Columbus from his third voyage, after word had got back to them that the Native Indians had been mistreated and the crew mismanaged by Columbus. He was recalled back to Spain by the King and Queen to explain the accusations of him wanting to make the natives his slaves. The King and Queen of Spain did not approve of slaves. Columbus explained to the King and Queen what had happened in the New World. All charges were removed and Columbus was set free to sail again.

Stamp issued in 1893

Isabella Pledging Her Jewels

The King and Queen of Spain first refused the expenses of Columbus' first voyage because of the war with the Moors, and because Spain was financially exhausted. After the war Queen Isabella said, "I will undertake the enterprise from my own Crown of Castile and will pledge my jewels to raise the necessary funds." Queen Isabella offered her jewels but it was not necessary; the Holy Brotherhood of Spain sponsored Columbus' voyage to the New World.

Stamp issued in 1893

Columbus in Chains

When Columbus was recalled from his third voyage and brought back to Spain in chains, he was charged with losing control of the *Santa María*, brutality, and of slave trading. The King and Queen of Spain did not approve of the taking of slaves from the newly discovered lands. They recalled Columbus because they wanted him to explain the accusations against him. Don Francisco de Bobadilla, the advocate for human treatment of the Indigenous people, began investigating the charges against Columbus. After Columbus' actions were investigated, he was set free and vindicated of all charges. He was then allowed to return back to sea in 1502.

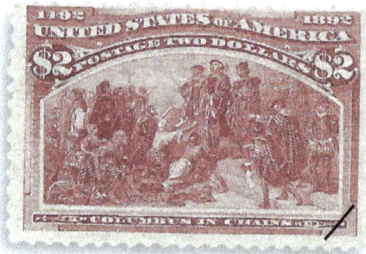

Stamp issued in 1893

Columbus Describing Third Voyage

From 1496 to 1497 Columbus was engaged in restoring his reputation before the courts of Spain. He needed to clear himself of accusations that arose against him from his first voyage. After the courts ruled that Columbus was cleared of his wrongdoing, he was permitted by the King and Queen to embark on his next voyage.

Stamp issued in 1893

During his third voyage, Columbus explored what are now the countries of Honduras, Nicaragua, Costa Rica and Panama before sailing back to *Hispaniola*, where he was marooned for one year. After being rescued, he returned to Spain on November 7, 1504.

Isabella and Columbus

Stamp issued in 1992

The first woman and Spaniard to be on a United States stamp was Queen Isabella I (1451-1504) of Castile, Spain with Christopher Columbus (1451-1506) for his great seamanship. The stamp was issued in 1893. With Queen Isabella's financial support, the discovery of the New World was possible. This would not have happened if the Queen of Spain had not supported Columbus. Originally Columbus was looking for a sea route to the Orient but in his voyage he located the Americas, the New World instead. Queen Isabella had pledged her Crown Jewels to finance the voyage, but when they received other financing, it was not necessary. Queen Isabella's decision to support Columbus was one of her best achievements as Queen. The discovery of the New World brought power to Spain and positioned the country as the leading country of explorers.

Columbus

Christopher Columbus (1451-1506), was an Italian explorer who crossed the Atlantic Ocean four times. He was always searching for a permanent settlement for Spain. In 1485, Columbus presented a request to the King of Portugal for the funding of the three ships and crew that he needed. His plan was to search for a sea route to the Orient but his request was denied. Columbus eventually did get his request from the King and Queen of Spain. In 1492 Columbus set foot on the Island of San Salvador in what is now called the Bahamas. Because of Columbus' voyage to the New World, he opened up the Americas for other explorers, but the Italian navigator was originally searching for a sea route to the Orient.

Stamp issued in 1992

Columbus Souvenir Sheets

The following six Voyages of Columbus Souvenir Sheets are reproductions of the original stamps from the Columbus Exposition of 1893, issued in 1992 to honor the 500th anniversary of Christopher Columbus' voyage and landing in the New World on October 12, 1492. The six sheets included in the following three pages are titled: Christopher Columbus, Seeking Royal Support, First Sighting of Land, Claiming a New World, Reporting Discoveries, and Royal Favor Restored.

*T*he United States Postal Service celebrates the 500th anniversary of the voyages of Christopher Columbus. This set is based on the first U.S. stamps in commemorative format, engraved a century ago.

Christopher Columbus

The Voyages of Columbus

Seeking Royal Support

HISPANIC HERITAGE AND PARTICIPATION ON UNITED STATES STAMPS

The Voyages of Columbus

First Sighting of Land

The Voyages of Columbus

Claiming a New World

EXPLORERS

HISPANIC HERITAGE AND PARTICIPATION ON UNITED STATES STAMPS

Vasco Núñez de Balboa

Stamp issued in 1913

Vasco Núñez de Balboa (1475-1519), born in Jerez de los Caballeros, Castile, Spain was a Spanish explorer and governor. Early in life, he wanted to be a sea explorer and a fencing champion. He led the first European land expedition from the Isthmus of Panama to the Pacific Ocean. Balboa was the first explorer to see the Pacific Ocean from a mountaintop and claimed the land for Spain in 1513. In 1915, the Panama-Pacific Exposition held in San Francisco, California, commemorated the discovery of the Pacific Ocean, as well as the building of the Panama Canal.

Coronado Expedition

Stamp issued in 1940

Francisco Vázquez de Coronado (1510-1545), Spanish explorer and conquistador, led the first expedition through present-day Arizona, New Mexico, Texas, Oklahoma, Kansas and throughout the American Southwest between 1540 and 1542. He was searching for the Seven Cities of Cibola, a legend he and his men had heard about. The men of Coronado's expedition were the first to see the Grand Canyon and ancient Pueblo villages that were built by the Hopi and the Zuni Indians. The path they took would later be called the Santa Fe Trail. In the end, no cities of gold were found, and Coronado returned empty-handed and in debt.

Juan Ponce de León

Juan Ponce de León (1460-1521), Spanish sailor and explorer, discovered Florida and claimed the land for Spain. He landed on the east coast, at a place that is now called Saint Augustine. He began his career in 1493 as a member of Christopher Columbus' second voyage to the New World. In 1508 and 1509, he explored and settled in Puerto Rico, founding the island's oldest settlement, Caparra, which today is known as the Pueblo Viejo sector of Guaynabo, just to the west of the present San Juan metropolitan area. Ponce de León served as the Island's first Governor. He wanted to discover the legendary Fountain of Youth. He never did, but his journey led him to discover Florida in 1513.

Stamp issued in 1982

Juan Rodríguez Cabrillo

Juan Rodríguez Cabrillo (1499-1543), a Portuguese explorer, was one of the first Europeans to explore the coastline of California. His nationality has been debated for centuries. Some believe he was born in Portugal, but others believe he was born in Seville, Spain. In 1542, he landed at San Diego Bay, a very good enclosed port, and named it San Miguel. The name was changed to San Diego 60 years later by explorer Sebastián Vizcaíno. Cabrillo discovered Santa Catalina Island and named it San Salvador, after his flagship. Later, he came to San Pedro Bay and named it *Baya de los Fumos* ("Smoke Bay").

Stamp issued in 1992

Cabrillo sailed the north coast of California and passed San Francisco. He failed to see it because of the fog. Many parks, schools and streets in California are named after him. In Southern California in San Pedro, Cabrillo Beach is named after him and September 28 is formally known as Cabrillo Day in San Diego.

Spanish Settlement

Don Juan de Oñate (1550-1626), was a Spanish conquistador and explorer. In 1598, Oñate traveled the first European road in the United States, *El Camino Real de Tierra Adentro* ("The Royal Road to the Interior Land"), which was 1,600 miles long, starting from Mexico City to Santa Fe, New Mexico. Later, he built the first European settlement west of the Mississippi River known as La Mission de San Miguel de San Gabriel, which is located in present day Española, New Mexico. He was the first Colonial Governor of the New Spain province of New Mexico, San Juan Pueblo.

Stamp issued in 1998

World Columbian Stamp Expo '92

The World's Columbian Exposition, also known as the Chicago World's Fair, was held in Chicago in 1893 to celebrate the 400th anniversary of Christopher Columbus arriving in the New World. The exposition was a big hit because in 1871 the city of Chicago had recovered from the Great Chicago Fire. October 9th of each year is known as "Chicago Day." It took three years of planning and preparation to put the World Columbus Exposition together. The dedication ceremonies were held on October 21, 1892, but the fairgrounds did not open until May 1, 1893, and closed on October 30, 1893. This was the first successful United States World Fair.

Stamp issued in 1993

Military

In every war, even before the American Revolutionary War to the present, Hispanic men and women proudly served to protect our nation, the United States of America. Throughout all of our wars, 61 Hispanics have been awarded the Congressional Medal of Honor, the highest award given for military bravery, presented to its recipient by the President of the United States of America in the name of Congress.

In World War II, Marine Pfc. Guy (Gabby) Louis Gabaldon, a U.S. Marine, was given the nickname "The Pied Piper of Saipan" or "Lone Wolf," because he single-handedly captured 1,300 (or 1,550 according to other sources) Japanese soldiers and civilians at Saipan and Tinian islands.

In Silvis, Illinois over 100 Latino men and women who had lived on Second Street served in the United States military forces since World War II. Nowhere in U.S. history had that many men and women who served in the armed forces come from a block and a half of the same street. The name Second Street was changed to "Hero Street, USA" in their honor. In May 1967, a city park was built and was named Hero Street Park.

The total number of Hispanic men and women who served in all the wars will never be known, because there were many Hispanics who did not have a Hispanic surname.

Medal of Honor

The Medal of Honor is the official name —often referred to as the Congressional Medal of Honor— for a military decoration created during the American Civil War, and is the highest military award for valor in combat for "courage above and beyond the call of duty." The medal is awarded by the President of the United States, and is only given to U.S. military personnel. There are three versions of the Medal: Army, Navy, and Air Force. Marines and Coast Guard receive the medal from the Navy.

Stamp issued in 1983

Sixty-one Hispanics have received the Medal of Honor:

    Three in the American Civil War

    One in the Boxer Rebellion War

    One in World War I

    Seventeen in World War II

    Fifteen in the Korean War

    Twenty-three in the Vietnam War

    One in the Afghanistan War

Civil War

RECIPIENT BRANCH BIRTH
Bazaar, Philip S. | Navy 1865 Chile

De Castro, Joseph H. | Army 1864 Boston, MA

Ortega, Juan | Navy 1864 Spain

BOXER REBELLION
Silva, France | Marine 1900 Hayward, CA

World Wars

WORLD WAR I
David, Barkley | Army 1918 Laredo, TX

WORLD WAR II
Adams, Lucian | Army 1944 Port Arthur, TX

Cano, Pedro | Army 1944 La Morita, Mexico

Davila, Rudolph | Army 1944 El Paso, TX

Gandara, Joe | Army 1944 Los Angeles, CA

García, Marcario | Army 1944 Sugar Land, TX

Gonsalves, Harold | Marine 1945 Alameda, CA

Gonzalez, David M. | Army 1945 Pacoima, CA

Herrera, Silvestre S. | Army 1945 El Paso, TX

Lara, Salvador | Army 1944 Riverside, CA

Lopez, José M. | Army 1944 Mission, TX

Martinez, Joe P. | Army 1943 Taos, NM

Perez, Manuel Jr. | Army 1945 Chicago, IL

Mendoza, Manuel V. | Army 1944 Miami, AZ

Rodríguez, Cleto L. | Army 1945 San Marcos, TX

Ruiz, Alejandro R. | Army 1945 Loving, NM

Valdez, José F. | Army 1945 Governador, NM

Villegas, Ysmael R. | Army 1945 Casa Blanca, CA

Wars

KOREA

Baldonado, Joe R. | Army 1950 Tampa, FL

Espinoza, Victor H. | Army 1952 El Paso, TX

García, Fernando Luis | Marine 1952 Utuado, P.R.

Gomez, Edward | Marine 1951 Omaha, NE

Gomez, Eduardo C. | Army 1950 Los Angeles, CA

Guillen, Ambrosio | Marine 1953 La Junta, CO

Hernández, Rodolfo P. | Army 1951 Colton, CA

López, Baldomero | Marine 1950 Tampa, FL

Martinez, Benito | Army 1952 Fort Hancock, TX

Negrón, Juan E. | Army 1951 Corozal, P.R.

Obregon, Eugene A. | Marine 1950 Los Angeles, CA

Pena, Mike C. | Army 1950 Newgulf, TX

Rivera, Demensio | Army 1951 Cabo Rojo, P.R.

Rodríguez, Joseph C. | Army 1950 San Bernardino, CA

Vera, Miguel A. | Army 1952 Adjuntas, P.R.

VIETNAM
Alvarado, Leonard L. | Army 1969 Bakersfield, CA

Baca, John P. | Army 1971 Providence, RI

Benavidez, Roy P. | Army 1968 Cuero, TX

Conde Falcón, Félix | Army 1969 Juncos, P.R.

De La Garza, Emilio | Marine 1970 Chicago, IL

Dias, Ralph E. | Marine 1969 Shelocta, PA

Duran, Jesus S. | Army 1977 Juarez, Mexico

Erevia, Santiago J. | Army Nordheim, TX

Fernandez, Daniel | Army 1966 Albuquerque, NM

Garcia, Candelario | Army 2013 Corsicana, TX

Gonzalez, Alfredo Cantu | Marine 1968 Edinburg, TX

Jiménez, José F. | Marine 1969 Mexico City, Mexico

Keith, Miguel | Marine 1970 San Antonio, TX

Lozada, Carlos J. | Army 1970 Caguas, P.R.

Rascon, Alfred V. | Army 2000 Chihuahua, Mexico

Rocco, Louis R. | Army 1970 Albuquerque, NM

Rodela, José | Army Corpus Christi, TX

Rubio, Eurípides | Army 1966 Ponce, P.R.

Santiago-Colón, Héctor | Army 1968 Salinas, P.R.

Rodrigues, Elmelindo S. | Army 1967 Honolulu, HA

Vargas, Jay R. | Marine 1968 Winslow, AZ

Yabes, Maximo | Army 1967 Lodi, CA

AFGHANISTAN
Petry, Leroy | Army 2001 Santa Fe, NM

David G. Farragut

Admiral David G. Farragut (1801-1870), was Spanish Scots-Irish. He was the son of Jorge and Elizabeth Farragut. He was sent to live with and was adopted by Capt. David Porter. He changed his original first name *James* to *David* in honor of his adoptive father. The adoption made David Farragut the foster brother of the famous Civil War Admiral James Dixon Porter.

Stamp issued in 1995

Farragut was the first Navy Admiral. At the age of nine, he was a midshipman; at the age of 12, he fought in the War of 1812. He was the first Navy Rear Admiral, and the first Vice Admiral. He was the Navy Commander for the North during the Civil War. Capturing New Orleans in the Battle of Mobile Bay earned him a place in history as one of America's most celebrated Civil War heroes. At the Battle of Mobile Bay his words shouted in the heat of battle, "Damn the torpedoes, full speed ahead," became famous, and have been used as a battle cry in other wars since then. His career lasted for 40 years.

Farragut & Porter

David G. Farragut and James Porter were both Civil War Naval Commanders. Farragut was the adopted brother of James Porter. Farragut's father was a son of Spanish-American immigrants, and the descendant of Conquistador Don Pedro Farragut, who served the King of Aragon. During the Battle of Mobile Bay in 1864, David Farragut led his fleet through the fields of torpedoes, and shouted, "Damn the torpedoes, full speed ahead." The Farragut family always had a big Navy tradition for generations. In 1866, Farragut was the first Navy Admiral, and his brother James Porter, became Vice Admiral at the same time.

Stamp issued in 1937

General Bernardo de Gálvez

General Bernardo de Gálvez (1746-1786) was a Spanish military leader and explorer. At the very young age of 16 he fought with Spain for the invasion of Portugal. With his knowledge in military studies, he also aided the American Thirteen Colonies, and helped win the American Revolutionary War from Great Britain. His forces consisted of Spaniards, Mexicans, Puerto Ricans and Cubans. With his brilliant knowledge in military warfare, General Gálvez helped win the battle against the British in Louisiana and Florida. He became Colonial Governor of Louisiana and Cuba.

Stamp issued in 1980

The city of Galveston, Texas is named in his honor for his contributions during the American Revolution. New Orleans named a street after him, Gálvez Street.

Civil War

During the Civil War, fought in the United States from 1861 to 1865, many Latinos were divided on both sides of the war. Approximately 2,550 Latinos joined the Confederates and 1,000 joined the Union forces. By 1864, there were over 10,000 Latinos fighting in the Civil War. While a large number of books have been written about the Civil War, there are few about Latinos in the Civil War. *Vaqueros in Blue and Gray*, and *Tejanos in Gray* are two books about the role of Latinos in the Civil War.

Colonel Miguel E. Pino, from the state of New Mexico, served as commander of the 2nd Regiment of volunteers from this state. There were other Mexican-American commanders like Lt. Colonel Chávez, who commanded a New Mexico militia unit, and General Stanislaus Montoya, who commanded one from Socorro County, New Mexico.

The state of Texas had 12 companies of Mexican-American Cavalry. One was the First Regiment of Texas Cavalry (Union). Other Mexican-American Texans (Tejanos) who served in the Civil War were Captain George Trevino, Clemente Zapata,

Stamp issued in 1962

Stamp issued in 1963

Stamp issued in 1964

Stamp issued in 1965

Cesario Falcon, and José Maria Martinez; also Lieutenants Ramon Garcia Falcon, Antonio Abad Dias, Santos Cadena and Cecilio Vela.

One Latina American patriot, whose bravery was noticed in the Civil War, was a woman named Loreta Janeta Velázquez. She was Cuban-American. She, along with other women, contributed to Civil War military history. Velázquez masqueraded as a Confederate soldier, enlisting in 1860 without her soldier-husband's knowledge. Serving as a spy she wore both male and female clothing. She fought at the Battle of Bull Run, Ball's Bluff and Fort Donelson. She was detected as a woman in New Orleans and discharged. She re-enlisted and fought at the Battle of Shiloh until she was again discovered as a woman.

Rough Riders

Many Mexican-Americans served as Rough Riders with Theodore Roosevelt. Among them were:

Private John B. Alamia

Private G.W. Aringo

Private José M. Baca

Private Frank C. Brito

Private José Brito

Private Abel B. Duran

Private Joseph L. Duran

Sergeant George W. Armijo

Captain Joe T. Sandoval

Stamp issued in 1948

Captain Maximiliano Luna was the most distinguished of the Rough Riders. He was a descendant from the conquistadors who settled in New Mexico in 1650. His family lived near the Rio Grande River since the 17th century. He was educated at Georgetown University in Washington D.C. Prior to joining the Rough Riders he was the sheriff in Valencia County, New Mexico.

Buffalo Soldiers

The Buffalo Soldiers have a very long history in the United States Army. They were members of the U.S. 9th and 10th Cavalry Regiment. Their unit was formed on September 21, 1866. Their nickname Buffalo Soldiers came from the Native American Indians.

One of those Buffalo Soldiers was Latino, Edward "Sancho" Mazique (1849-1951). Mazique was born a slave in Columbia, South Carolina. Even though they were French Creole, Mazique and his family were

Stamp issued in 1994

owned by the Widow Green family, and were given to Dr. Edward Fleming as a gift. Mazique joined the Army February 23, 1875, and was placed in the 10th Black Cavalry Regiment, Company E. In 1880, he was honorably discharged at Fort Concho. At the age of 101, Sancho fell and broke his arm. While he was healing he caught pneumonia and died.

Battleship Maine

Stamp issued in 1998

The USS Maine (ACR-1), was a battleship named after the state of Maine that was sent to Cuba in 1898 to help protect American interests, and to support Cuban independence. On February 15, 1893, the USS Maine was rocked by explosions while in the harbor of Havana. More than 250 American sailors were killed. In support of the war against Spain, Admiral David Farragut, while leading the fleet into the harbor of Havana yelled, "Damn the torpedoes, full speed ahead." It later became a famous battle cry and slogan. Two months after the sinking of the Maine, America declared war on Spain.

World War I

World War I was an international conflict fought in Central Europe between 1914 and 1918, and involved many great countries. Over 200,000 Hispanic men and women served in World War I. Only one Hispanic received the Medal of Honor, and only one was an Ace in World War I.

Stamp issued in 1985

Army Private David B. Barkley (1899-1918) was the Army's only Hispanic to receive the Medal of Honor in WWI. He used his Anglo father's last name, Josef Barkley, to avoid discrimination in the military. He grew up with his Mexican-American mother, Antonia Cantu, after his parents separated. General Pershing presented the *Medal of Honor* to Barkley's mother at her home in San Antonio, Texas in 1919. His Mexican-American background was noticed in 1918, at the time of his death, but it wasn't until 1989 —71 years after he gave his life for his country— that he was fully recognized as being Mexican-American. Private Barkley was born in Laredo, Texas. France awarded him the *Croix de Guerre*, and Italy the *Croce al Merito di Guerra*.

Capt. Ralph (Rodolfo) Ambrose O'Neill (1896-1980) was a Mexican-American World War Ace. He was born in Durango, Durango, Mexico, with dual citizenship of the United States and Mexico. He was born to an American-Irish father, Ralph Lawrence O'Neill, and Mexican mother, Dolores Petra Avila. His family moved to Nogales, Arizona in 1901. During World War I he was assigned to the 147th Aero Squadron, in France, flying the biplane fighter aircraft Nieuport 28 and other aircraft. He shot down five German aircraft in aerial combat. He was awarded the Distinguished Service Cross with *two Oak Leaf Clusters* and the *Croix de Guerre*. After World War I, he returned back to Mexico, training the Mexican Air Force fighter pilots.

World War II

World War II was a global war that lasted from 1939 to 1945, involving more than 30 countries and resulting in more than 50 million military and civilian deaths. Over 500,000 Hispanic men and women served in WWII. The war was fought in the Southeast jungles of Asia, North African deserts, Pacific Islands, Atlantic beaches and in the streets of Europe. Seventeen Hispanics received the Congressional Medal of Honor.

Stamp issued in 1998

Capt. Donald S. Lopez (1923-2008) was a volunteer pilot in the U.S. Army Air Corps with the 23rd Fighter Group in China and Burma. Capt. Lopez flew Curtis P-40's and the P-51's as a Flying Tiger. He became an "Ace" after shooting down 5 Japanese aircraft in aerial combat. In Korea he flew the F-86, a transonic jet fighter aircraft. Six Latino Americans became flying Aces in WWII. To become an Ace, pilots required a number of aerial victories.

Marine Pfc. Guy Louis Gabaldon "Gabby" (1926-2006), became known as "The Pied Piper of Saipan." He was a Mexican-American from East Los Angeles. At the age of 18 he joined the United States Marine Corps, and served in World War II at Saipan. At a very early age he knew many Japanese-American families, and they taught him the Japanese language. Sadly, his Japanese-American friends and their families were sent to Heart Mountain Relocation Center in Wyoming. At Saipan, he single-handedly captured between 1,300 and 1,500 —depending on the source— Japanese soldiers and civilians because he was able to talk the Japanese into surrendering. He was nominated for the Congressional Medal of Honor, but was awarded the Silver Star, then upgraded to the Navy Cross. A movie was made about him capturing Japanese soldiers and civilians. The film was called *Hell to*

Eternity. The movie does not acknowledge that Marine Pfc. Gabaldon was Mexican-American.

During World War II, one of the allies in the war was Mexico. *The "Escuadrón Aéreo de Pelea 201"* was a Mexican fighter squadron that aided the allied war effort during World War II. The squadron was also known by the nickname of Águilas Aztecas or "Aztec Eagles." The Mexican Air Force flew the P-49 Thunderbolt fighter aircraft. They were attached to the 58th Fighter Group in the Philippines with 96 combat missions, 300 ground crew, including 30 experienced pilots. One of the pilots was Carlos Faustino (Charles Foster), a fighter pilot Ace from Mexico; he flew along with American pilots. He flew 25 missions and was awarded the *La Cruz de Honor* or "Cross of Honor," equivalent to the United States Congressional Medal of Honor.

Classic American Aircraft P-51 Mustang

During World War II, the P-51 Mustang Airplanes were flown by the Tuskegee African-American fighter pilots, who flew with the 332nd Fighter Group, and the 477th Bombardment Group United States Air Force. The Tuskegee Airman pilots were also known as the Red Tails after they painted the tails of their aircraft red.

Stamp issued in 1997

There were Hispanics who flew and served with the Tuskegee Airmen, among them fighter pilot Second Lieutenant Esteban Hotesse, a Dominican. Lt. Hotesse was one of 103 African American Officers who were arrested for entering the Officer Club. He and his family immigrated to the United States from Moca, Dominican Republic, at the age of four. Other Hispanics who were Puerto Ricans were TSgt Eugene Calderon, Company Clerk, and TSgt Pablo Diaz Albortt, Special Service Office.

Korean War

In 1950, the North Korean forces crossed the 38th parallel and attacked South Korea. Nearly 148,000 Hispanic men and women served in the Korean War. Fifteen Hispanics received the Congressional Medal of Honor.

Air Force Capt. Manuel J. Fernandez, Jr., a fighter pilot Ace, flew 125 combat missions in the Korean War. He shot down 14 MIG-15 fighter aircraft, all within his first nine months. Capt. Fernandez was the third leading Ace in Korea, and was awarded the Distinguished Flying Cross and the Silver Star.

Stamp issued in 1985

Stamp issued in 1999

Stamp issued in 2003

Vietnam

The United States involvement in the Vietnam War was to help stop North Vietnam communists from entering and capturing South Vietnam. From 1955 to 1975, 58,195 men and women sacrificed their lives. Initially, the Vietnam War was called a Cold War conflict, which took place in South Vietnam, Laos and Cambodia. Military advisors arrived in the 1950s, and then the conflict escalated in the early 1960s, reaching the peak of the War in 1968, at the time of the Tet Offensive, with many fatalities throughout Vietnam.

The Vietnam Veterans Memorial Wall, also called "The Black Wall," has the names of all the men and women in order by the date they lost their lives. Approximately 1,200 of the names on the Wall are MIA's or POW's, (Missing in Action or Prisoners of War). It's a place to honor, to heal and remember. The Vietnam Memorial Wall began construction on March 26, 1982 and opened to the public on November 14, 1982, with thousands of visitors for the dedication the first day.

At the age of 20, Maya Ying Lin, an Asian-American Yale University undergraduate student, was selected to design the Vietnam Veterans Memorial.

Stamp issued in 1979

Stamp issued in 1999

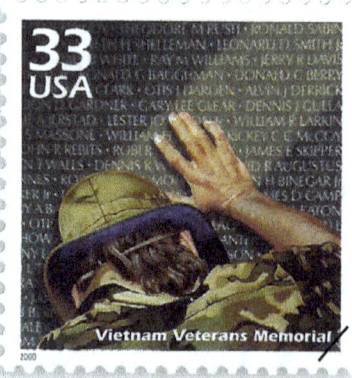

Stamp issued in 2000

There were 1,421 entries in the contest to design the memorial.

Over 200,000 Hispanic men and women served in Vietnam. Twenty-three Hispanic military personnel received the Congressional Medal of Honor in Vietnam.

Stamp issued in 1984

Captain Maria Luisa Ayala Mellman, a Mexican-American "Angel in Olive Drab," served with the Army Combat Nurse Corps with the 12th Evacuation Hospital at Cú Chi South Vietnam from 1968 to 1969. Captain Mellman was awarded the Army Commendation Medal for her service in Vietnam. She is from Chandler, Arizona and graduated from Arizona State University receiving her BSN in Nursing. After her military service, she continued working in Hospitals in the Public Health sector. She worked 19 years as a certificated school nurse. Nursing personnel in Vietnam usually wore lightweight olive drab fatigues made of cotton poplin.

Women in the Armed Services

For the past 400 years to the present, Hispanic women have proudly served in our military. The number of women who served in all U.S. wars are:

Stamp issued in 1952

400 in American Revolutionary War

35,000 in World War I

500,000 in World War II

120,000 in the Korean War

7,500 in the Vietnam War

44,000 in the Gulf War

In the American Civil War there were three Latina American sisters who served as spies. The Sánchez sisters were Cuban. Maria Dolores (Lola), Francesca (Panchita), and Eugenia, were Confederate women spies. At parties or at gatherings, the Sanchez sisters overheard important information from the Union soldiers about their plans for raids. The Sanchez sisters gathered their information and passed it on to the Confederates. Lola went on horseback and notified the Confederates about the plans for raids. This information surprised the Union, as it resulted in the capture of the USS Columbine, a Union war ship. This became known as the Battle of Horse Landing.

Another spy was Loreta Janeta Velázquez, a Cuban. She dressed as a male Confederate soldier to get secret information.

Carmen Contreras Bozak, a Puerto Rican, was the first Hispanic woman to serve in the Women's Army Auxiliary Corps (WAAC) in 1942. Being bilingual, she joined as a cryptologist for the 149th WAAC Post Headquarters Company, and went overseas to North Africa in 1943.

Sergeant Mary (Valfre) Castro was the first Mexican-American from San Antonio, Texas to join the WAAC. She joined the WAAC in World War II, and was selected as a Sergeant in the new Women's Army Corps (WAC) as a drill Sergeant. Castro joined to help seven members of her family who were fighting in WWII. She served in the Southwest Pacific.

Hometowns Honor Their Returning Veterans, 1945

After World War II, all Veterans returning home were treated to a hero's welcome. There were parades and celebrations across America to show support for our men and women, including the wounded and the disabled. Over 500,000 Hispanic men and women served in WWII. Thirteen Hispanics were awarded the Medal of Honor.

Stamp issued in 1995

MILITARY

POW-MIA

The POW-MIA flag was created as a remembrance for the men and women in combat who are a Prisoner of War or Missing in Action. From the Civil War to the present, these are the number of POW-MIA's in each war:

Stamp issued in 1995

Civil War, Union and Confederacy — 309,608

World War I — 7,479

World War II — 154,383

Korean War — 15,317

Vietnam War — 2,583

Invasion of Grenada — 4

Persian Gulf War — 52

The Prisoner of War-Missing in Action (POW-MIA) flag was designed and created in 1971 by the National League of Families. The motto is "You Are Not Forgotten."

In 1942, during World War II, two National Guard units —the 200th and the 515th Battalions— from New Mexico, Arizona, and Texas, of Spanish-speaking military, were sent to Clark Air Base in the Philippine Islands. Hispanic and non-Hispanic soldiers were captured by the Japanese Imperial Army, and forced to march 5 to 10 days the 60 to 69-mile in the Bataan Death March, from Bataan to the Japanese prison camps.

Colonel Virgilio N. Cordero Jr. (1893–1980) was one of nearly 1,600 infantry who were taken as prisoners; half of these men perished. After the war, Col.Cordero retired as rank of Brigadier General, and wrote about his experiences during the Bataan Death March in the book, *My Experiences* during the War with Japan, published in 1950. In 1957, he wrote a Spanish version titled, *Bataan y la Marcha de la Muerte*.

Ralph Rodriguez Jr., Private, (1917-2017), of the 200th Coast Artillery Battalion, was a Bataan Death March survivor who served as a medic. After the war, he was the National Commander of the Bataan Veterans Organization, and of the American Ex-Prisoners of War.

Agapito E. "Gap" Silva Corporal (1919–2007) was a member of the 200th Battalion who also survived the Bataan Death March in the Philippines.

Everett Alvarez, Jr., a Mexican-American Navy LTJG, served in Vietnam. Alvarez was the first American fighter pilot to be shot down and held as a POW in North Vietnam. He was held for 8 years 7 months, and is the second longest held POW in American history. Alvarez was awarded the Silver Star, two Legion of Merit medals, two Bronze Stars, the Distinguished Flying Cross, and two Purple Hearts. Alvarez has written two books, *Chained Eagle* and *Code of Conduct*.

Women in Military Service

Women in military have been serving the United States in the U.S. Army, Navy, Marines, Air Force and Coast Guard. These women are of different diversity of all races and culture: Hispanic, African, White, Asian, and Native Americans.

Stamp issued in 1997

American women have been serving in the military since the American Revolution War to the present. The Women in the Military Services Memorial at Arlington National Cemetery is for honoring the many military women from the past, present and the future. It's the only major national memorial honoring women who served in all the wars. The monument was dedicated October 18, 1997.

Lori Ann Baca Piestewa (Kocha-Hon-Mana her Hopi name), was the first Native American (Hopi/Mexican) woman in history to die in combat in 2003 in the invasion of Iraq. Her father is Terry Piestewa, a full-blooded Hopi and a Vietnam veteran, and her mother is Priscilla "Percy" Baca, a Mexican-American. Arizona's Piestewa Peak is named in her honor.

Honoring Those Who Served Desert Storm, Desert Shield

The Gulf War, codenamed Operation Desert Shield during the operations conducted to the buildup of troops and defense of Saudi Arabia, and Operation Desert Storm in its combat phase, lasted from August 2, 1990 to February 28, 1991. The Gulf War was to help defend Saudi Arabia in the Persian Gulf after the invasion of Kuwait. The Gulf War was led by the United States and 35 coalition forces against Iraq in response to Iraq's invasion and annexation of Kuwait.

Capt. Manuel Rivera Jr. (1959-1991), a Marine aviator, was the first Latino killed in Operation Desert Shield. Capt. Rivera was killed over the Persian Gulf in his AV-8B Harrier.

Stamp issued in 1991

Over 20,000 Hispanic men and women served in Operation Desert Shield, Desert Storm.

Gulf War

The Persian Gulf War was an international conflict triggered by Iraq's invasion of Kuwait on August 2, 1990. During this war hundreds of oil wells were set on fire and oil was dumped in the Persian Gulf. The Iraqis were eventually defeated and driven out of Kuwait. Over 20,000 Hispanic men and women served in the Gulf War.

Stamp issued in 2000

Hostages Come Home

The American Embassy at Tehran, Iran was taken over by the Iranians from November 4, 1979 to January 20, 1981, for a total of 444 days. This diplomatic standoff between Iran and the United States is known as the Iran hostage crisis. A total of 65 military and government employees were held captive during this time. After their release on January 21, 1981, all 65 Americans were taken to West Germany. On January 27, 1981 they all arrived at Andrews Air Force Base, in the United States, and were given a hero's welcome.

Stamp issued in 2000

At the time, two Mexican-American United States Marines, Sgt. James M. Lopez, from Globe, Arizona, and Corp. Anthony Gallegos, from Pueblo, Colorado, were both serving in the Marine Security Guards Detachment in the United States Embassy in Teheran. Both were awarded the Prisoner of War Medal.

Events

Hispanic history, culture and events in the United States existed for hundreds of years before the Anglos began migrating to America from Europe. Stretching back to the Pre-Revolutionary War Era, Hispanics were present. Mexicans became the first American citizens in the newly acquired Southwest Territory after the Mexican-American War (1846-1848).

Spanish explorer Vasco Núñez de Balboa crossed the Isthmus of Panama to the Pacific Ocean in 1513. He is considered the first European to lead an expedition to have seen or reached the Pacific from the New World.

In 1790, Spanish explorer Salvador Fidalgo, sailing north along the California coastline, reached the Alaska coastline and named the area Puerto Córdova, and the Port of Valdez, Alaska, which was named in 1790 after the Spanish Navy Minister Antonio Valdés y Fernández Bazán.

Panama Canal

The Panama Canal was built to connect the Atlantic Ocean to the Pacific Ocean, saving over 8,000 miles from sailing around South America. The canal is 48-miles long. The French began the construction in 1881 but failed to complete it. In 1904 the United States began construction and completed the canal in 1914, at a cost of $375 million dollars. The first ship to pass through the Panama Canal was the United States cargo ship the Ancon. The Panama-Pacific Exposition was held in San Francisco commemorating the discovery of the Pacific Ocean as well as the construction of the Panama Canal.

Stamp issued in 1913

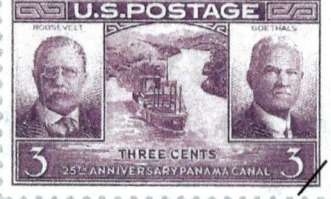

Stamp issued in 1939

Stamp issued in 1998

Golden Gate Bridge - San Francisco

The Golden Gate Bridge is one of the Wonders of the Modern World. Construction began in January 1933, and it cost more than 35 million dollars. It was completed in April 1937. It's the longest suspension bridge in the world, and is 4,200-feet long between the towers. In 1915, San Francisco was the Pacific stopover for many ships that passed

Stamp issued in 1913

through the Panama Canal going from the East to West Coasts. The San Francisco Harbor is the location from which most ships set sail across the Pacific bound for the Orient. Today, it's best known as the Golden Gate Bridge.

Pan American Union

The Pan American Union was first organized in 1890 and adopted in 1910. This was the first of the modern Inter-American Conferences, and there were representatives from all of Latin America and the United States. The first to organize a Pan American Union was Simón Bolívar in 1826. It was Bolívar's dream to unite South America with the United States. This stamp was created to commemorate the Good Neighbor Policy, implemented by President Franklin Roosevelt. Its purpose was to help promote cooperation between the United States and the countries of South America.

Stamp issued in 1940

Pony Express

The Pony Express mail service lasted only a short time, from 1860 to 1861. For 19 months, Pony Express riders delivered mail, packages, and newspapers from St. Joseph, Missouri to Sacramento, California on horseback. The riders were very young men who rode horses for the United States Post Office. They were called "The Pony Express Riders." There were 184 stations; each station was 10 miles apart, where each rider changed horses. They took the mail pouch called a *mochila* (backpack). Each *mochila* could carry 10 pounds of mail. Each rider was also given a Bible. The riders could not weigh over 125 pounds, and they rode day and night Their pay was $25.00 a week.

Stamp issued in 1940

Stamp issued in 1960

Below is a list of the few Hispanic Pony Express Riders:

    Juan Santo Avila from Redwing, Colorado

    Antonio Gonzales from Bexar County, Texas

    Pedro Pantaleon Gonzales from Taos County, Texas

    Hilario Saenz from La Mesa, New Mexico

    Quirino Saenz from La Mesa, New Mexico

    Juan De Dios Saenz from La Mesa, New Mexico

    Anastasio Villescas from Mesilla, New Mexico

Corregidor, Manila Bay

The Spanish established Manila Bay as a seaport in 1571. Called the "Gibraltar of the Pacific," Manila Bay is the most important seaport in the Philippines. For many centuries, the Philippines were ruled by Spain, Japan, and then the United States. They became the Republic of the Philippines in 1946. During World War II, Filipino troops played an important role in the United States land forces victory on the islands over the Japanese. The United States controlled the Philippines until 1935, when it was established as an independent commonwealth.

Stamp issued in 1944

Gadsden Purchase

The Gadsden Purchase was also known as the *Venta de La Mesilla* ("Sale of La Mesilla"). In 1853, James Gadsden, the U.S. Ambassador to Mexico, signed a treaty with Mexico to pay $10 million for a strip of land south of the Gila River and west of the Rio Grande, a 29,670 square mile region that is now part of the states of Arizona and New Mexico. The purpose of the land sale was to acquire the land needed to build the transcontinental railroad. For six years, both the United States and Mexico claimed the Mesilla Valley as their land. The Gadsden Purchase was the last sale of land to the United States and it created the southwestern boundary with Mexico.

Stamp issued in 1953

EVENTS

Carreta

The *carreta* (cart) was the principal mode of transportation used by many of the early Spanish and Mexican settlers throughout the Southwest. *Carretas* carried many people, including women and children, as they traveled for many miles seeking to find a better life. The carreta was used for transporting materials from different locations, hauling supplies, timber and other items the settlers needed. Oxen, horses, mules or donkeys pulled the *carretas*. The wheels were never greased because the people believed that the sound of the wheels squeaking would scare the evil spirits away. Many *carretas* were handmade of wood and with handmade tools. The large wheels made it easier to travel more smoothly over the rocky dirt roads. The carreta was eventually replaced by trucks, trains, and by other means of transportation. They are often seen in parades and festivals in celebrations of the past.

Stamp issued in 1988

Carmel Mission

Carmel Mission (San Carlos Borroméo del Río Carmelo) was named after Charles Borroméo, Archbishop of Milan, Italy. Father Junipero Serra began building missions across California and Carmel Mission was the second mission he built. In 1770, in the town of Monterey near the native village of Tamo, the Esselen and Ohlone Native Americans were taught to farm. They learned to plow, to be shepherds, cattle herders and blacksmiths. They also made adobe brick, tile and tools, all of which were used to build Carmel Mission. Father Junipero was buried beneath the chapel floor in 1784. Carmel Mission is on the National Register of Historic Places and a United States National Landmark.

Stamp issued in 1988

Music, Dance, Theater and Movies

Hispanic American men and women have entertained us in many ways—playing music, introducing different dances and performing in the theater. The first Hispanic entertainers in the U.S. laid the footprints for other Hispanics to follow.

Actress Myrtle Gonzalez, a native Latina and member of Californio-American family from Mexico, performed in 78 silent era motion pictures from 1913 to 1917.

Beatriz Michelena, a Venezuelan-American actress, was the leading lady in four of her silent movies between the 1910s and 1920s.

The Cisco Kid, a television series aired from 1950 to 1956, staring Duncan Renaldo as the *Cisco Kid*, and Leo Carrillo as *Pancho,* was about two Mexican Caballeros. At the end of every episode, one or the other would say as a joke "O, Pancho!" "O, Cisco!" with laughter.

Lydia Mendoza, a Mexican-American guitarist and singer of Tejano from Houston, Texas, known as "The First Lady of Tejano," recorded over 1,000 songs.

Selena Quintanilla-Perez, a Mexican-American singer and songwriter, known as "The Queen of Tejano Music," is one of the most celebrated Hispanic singers of the late 20th century.

Rita Dolores Moreno, a Puerto Rican-American, is the only actress, dancer and singer to win an Oscar, an Emmy, a Tony, and a Grammy. On December 6, 2015, Moreno received the 38th annual national Kennedy Center Honors Lifetime Artistic Achievement Award.

Linda Maria Ronstadt, a Mexican-American singer, has won 11 Grammy Awards, and three American Music Awards, among other awards. In 1987, Ronstadt's Spanish album *Canciones de Mi Padre* was released. In 2014, she was inducted into the Rock and Roll Hall of Fame, and in the same year she was awarded the National Medal of Arts and Humanities.

Gloria Estefan, a Cuban-American singer, songwriter, and actress. Her 1993 Spanish-language album *Mi Tierra* won the first of her three Grammy Awards for Best Tropical Latin Album. She has a Star on the Hollywood Walk of Fame and the Las Vegas Walk of Fame.

All these artists have one thing in common: to perform and entertain us.

John Philip Sousa

John Philip Sousa (1854-1932), was an American of Portuguese-Bavarian ancestry who became a famous American composer and bandmaster. He was born in Washington, D.C. His ability earned him the title "March King." In 1867, Sousa's father enlisted him in the Marines, at the very early age of 13, as an apprentice. Sousa was discharged from the Marines in 1875, but in 1880 he returned to lead the Marine Band. On December 25, 1896, he composed *The Stars and Stripes Forever*, which became the official marching song of the United States. Sousa toured with his band for 40 years all over the world. He composed 136 marching songs, 15 operettas, and 70 songs. In 1952, his biography was made into a movie. The name of the movie was *Stars and Stripes Forever*.

Stamp issued in 1940

Desi Arnaz

Desi Arnaz, born Desiderio Alberto Arnaz III (1917-1986), was a Cuban actor, musician and television producer. In 1933 his family fled Santiago, Cuba, because of a revolution led by Fulgencio Batista. He began working as a musician and joined the band of Xavier Cugat in New York. He later introduced a dance called the "Conga Line." It was such a hit that he started his own band. He was offered a role in the 1939 Broadway musical *Too Many Girls*, where he met his wife to be, Lucille Ball. Desi served in the U.S. Army during World War II, where he and other musicians entertained the troops. After the war, he was the orchestra leader on Bob Hope's radio show from 1946 to 1947. In 1950, Lucille and Desi founded Desilu Productions to produce and sell a television series. Their most popular show was called *I Love Lucy*. His role in the show was Ricky Ricardo, Lucy's husband. The show ran for many years, and it is still popular today. It became one of the most successful television programs in history.

MUSIC, DANCE, THEATER AND MOVIES

Let's Dance Merengue

The Merengue is a rural folk dance and music from the Dominican Republic. It was first mentioned around the middle of the 19th century, but the island's dictator Rafael Trujillo promoted the Merengue from 1930 to 1961, turning it into Dominican's national music and dance style. One of two versions about the origin of the genre asserts the slaves working in the sugar plantation fields to the beat of drums inspired the dance because they were connected to each other with chains strapped to their ankles, so when they walked they dragged one foot. Merengue was brought to the United States in the 1900s. Many years later the dance became a popular ballroom dance.

Stamp issued in 2005

The artist for *Let's Dance Merengue* is Rafael López. He also created other stamps: *Latin Music Legends* and *Mendez v. Westminster*.

Let's Dance Salsa

The Salsa is an Afro-Cuban dance which became an international dance. The dance originated in the Caribbean and became extremely popular in cities like Cali, Colombia, which is known as the *Capital de la Salsa*. In the United States, Salsa dance was popularized in part by the Cubans who migrated to Miami. The Salsa dance is performed mainly in Dominican Republic, Colombia, Puerto Rico, Mexico, New York, Central America, South America, Europe, but it is popular around the world.

Stamp issued in 2005

The artist for *Let's Dance Salsa* is José Ortega. Other stamps by him are: *With Love and Kisses* and *Garden of Love*.

Let's Dance Cha-Cha-Cha

The Cha-cha-cha is a dance from Cuba, and is a combination of the Mambo and American swing. Cha-cha-cha comes from very old traditions of Africa. In time it was called Afro-Cuban dance, and was developed by Enrique Jorrín, a composer and violinist, in Havana, Cuba in the 1950s. The dance became very popular in Cuba, Mexico and New York, and then spread across the United States. The Cha-cha-cha is a dance in many ballroom competitions around the world and it can be danced to Cuban music, any Latin pop or Latin rock music.

Stamp issued in 2005

The artist for *Let's Dance Cha-Cha-Cha* is Edel Rodriguez.

Let's Dance Mambo

Stamp issued in 2005

The Mambo is a mixture of Latin dances that came from the French and Spanish of the Caribbean Colonies. The word mambo means "conversation with the gods" in the Kongo language spoken by the slaves from Central Africa that were taken to Cuba. Mambo, as created by Cuban musician Dámaso Pérez Prado in the early 1940s, became very popular in Cuba, Mexico and New York. In time, the dance changed to what it is today, and Mambo at times is called Salsa. In the 1950s, New York's newspapers published many articles on what they called the "Mambo Revolution" music and dance. Once the word was out, Mambo dance spread throughout the United States and around the world.

The artist for Let's Dance Mambo is Sergio Baradat.

Carmen Miranda

Carmen Miranda, born Maria do Carmo Miranda da Cunha (1909-1955), was a Portuguese-born Brazilian samba singer, dancer, Broadway actress, and film star from the 1930s to 1950s. Nicknamed "The Brazilian Bombshell," she was very popular in Latin music with her fruit hats made of bananas and other fruits. She was also known as the "Lady in the Tutti-Frutti Hat." Carmen starred in the 1939 Broadway show *The Streets of Paris*, and in 14 films between 1940 and 1953. By 1945, Carmen was the highest paid woman performer in the U.S. movie industry making over $200,000 that year. In 1955, she had a heart attack and collapsed during a live performance on the *Jimmy Durante Show*. She died the next day at the age of 46. Her body was sent to her adopted country of Brazil, where the government declared a national day of mourning.

Stamp issued in 2010

Artist for Latin Music Legends is Rafael Lopez.

Selena

Selena Quintanilla-Perez (1971-1995), was a Mexican American singer. She began singing with her family band *Los Dinos*, with her sister Suzette and brother A.B. as members. She began performing at age nine, and recorded her first album at the age of 12, specializing in Tejano music. By age 23, she was on her way to stardom. In the months that followed Selena's death in 1995, the world got a chance to see what might have been. Her crossover album *Dreaming of You* was issued shortly after her death. It was a mix of Spanish and English songs. Selena was the Tejano Female Artist of the Decade for both the 1980s and the 1990s. In 1993, she won the Grammy Award for her Mexican-American album, *Selena, The Queen of Tejano Music*. On June 28, 2017, Selena posthumously received her star on the Hollywood Walk of Fame.

Stamp issued in 2010

Artist for Latin Music Legends is Rafael Lopez.

Carlos Gardel

Carlos Gardel, born Charles Romuald Gardés (1890-1935), was a French Argentine singer, songwriter, composer and actor. The Tango dance is often called the "Passion of Dance," and Gardel *was* the Tango. He influenced Latin American music and earned the nickname "King of the Tango." He also starred in European films. His films helped popularize the Tango. In 1917, he recorded the first Tango sung with lyrics, *Mi Noche Triste* (*My Sad Night*). The song was a smash hit. There were over 300 Tango songs. He died in a plane crash in Colombia in 1935.

Stamp issued in 2010

The artist for Latin Music Legends is Rafael Lopez.

Tito Puente

Ernesto Antonio "Tito" Puente (1923-2000), was a New-York born Puerto Rican musician, songwriter and record producer. In high school, Tito played with some of the hottest Latino bands in New York City, the *Machito Orchestra, Los Happy Boys*, and the *Brothers Morales Orchestra*. When Tito served in the U.S. Navy, he was in nine battles on the escort carrier USS Santee during WWII. After the war, Tito's new group was the *Piccadilly Boys*, which rose to the top of the mambo and salsa music. He became known as the "King of Latin Music," and also as "El Rey de los Timbales." In 1969, he received the Key to the City of New York for his music career.

Artist for Latin Music Legends is Rafael Lopez.

Celia Cruz

Úrsula Hilaria Celia de la Caridad Cruz Alfonso, better known as Celia Cruz (1925-2003), was a singer born in Havana, Cuba. Celia grew up in the Havana neighborhood of Santos Suarez. In the 1940s, she won a singing contest on the radio show *La hora del té* (*Tea Time*). Celia always told jokes when ordering her coffee. When asked, "Do you want sugar?" her reply was, "You can't have Cuban coffee without *azúcar*" (sugar), and that Spanish word became her well-known catch phrase. Celia played a major role in Salsa music across the United States and Latin America, and became known as the "Queen of Salsa." For many years Celia was the lead singer for *La Sonora Matancera,* an Afro-Cuban band. Some of her hits were *Quimbara*, *Tu voz*, and *Usted abusó*. She won 23 gold records with Tito Puente, the Fania All-Stars, and other musicians. Celia died of brain cancer at the age of 77.

Ritchie Valens

Richard Steven Valenzuela (1941-1959), was born in Pacoima, California. He was a Mexican-American singer, songwriter and guitarist, and was professionally known as Ritchie Valens. He learned to play the guitar and joined a band in high school. He was the first Chicano Rock and Roll star, and at the age of 16 he recorded the songs *Come On, Let's Go* and *Donna*. Donna was a girl he loved and he named the song after her. Another great hit song was *La Bamba*. Ritchie died at the age of 17, on February 3, 1959, along with fellow singers Buddy Holly and "The Big Bopper" (Jiles Perry Richardson, Jr.) in a plane crash in Iowa. A song was made to honor all three, *The Day the Music Died*. In 1990, Valens posthumously received a star on the Hollywood Walk of Fame. While his career lasted only eight months, he laid the footprints for other Mexican-American musicians to follow.

Latin Jazz

Stamp issued in 2008

From the early 1900s, musicians from the Caribbean islands and the United States joined together and created Latin jazz. By the 1930s, Latin jazz had spread across nightclubs in America. In the 1940s the big bands of Dizzy Gillespie and Machito, Tito Puente, Ray Barretto, Eddie Palmieri and others played Latin jazz across America and around the world. Latin jazz is also called Afro-Cuban jazz. Two classes of Latin jazz are Brazilian Latin jazz and Afro-Cuban Latin jazz, which include: Bossa Nova, Salsa, Merengue, Songo, Son, Mambo, Timba, Bolero, Charanga, and the Cha-cha-cha. The Latin jazz, also known as "Spanish tinge," started in New Orleans. The first Latin jazz piece was the *Tanga*.

The Latin Jazz stamp was designed by Michael Bartalos.

Lydia Mendoza

Stamp issued in 2013

Lydia Mendoza (1916-2007), was a singer and guitarist. She was born in Houston, Texas. Lydia is best known as "The First Lady of Tejano Music," and *La Alondra de la Frontera* (*The Lark of the Border*). Lydia began playing her 12-string guitar at a very early age in front of other family members. In 1928 Lydia and family members, the *Cuarteto Carta Blanca*, made their first recording. In 1934, she recorded *Mal Hombre* (*Evil Man*), an overnight success. She recorded more than a thousand songs in a career that lasted more than seven decades. Lydia received many awards. In 1982, she became the first Texan to receive the National Heritage Fellowship and the Lifetime Achievement Award from the National Endowment for the Arts. In 1999, she was awarded the National Medal of Arts, and in 2003 she was among the second group to be awarded the Texas Cultural Trust. She died on December 20, 2007, in San Antonio, Texas, at the age of 91.

Art director for the Lydia Mendoza stamp was Antonio Alcalá.

José Limón

José Arcadio Limón (1908-1972), was born in Culiacán, Sinaloa, Mexico. José Limón was a pioneer in dance and choreography. In 1915, he and his family moved from Mexico to Los Angeles, and then he moved to New York to study at the New York School of Design in 1928. In 1946, he began the José Limón Dance Company. In 1930, he choreographed his dance *Etude in D Minor*. In 1943, Limón was drafted into the U.S. Army, where he collaborated with composer Frank Loesser and Alex North for the Army Special Services. In 1946, Limón became a U.S. citizen. At the age of 64, Limón died from cancer. He was inducted into the National Museum of Dance.

Stamp issued in 2012

Lynda Jean Córdova Carter - *Wonder Woman*

Lynda Carter, born Lynda Jean Córdova Carter (1951), is a Mexican American-Irish actress. Her parents are Colby Carter and Juanita Córdova. Lynda was born in Phoenix, Arizona, and attended Globe High School, Arcadia High School, and Arizona State University. At the very early age of five, she made her first public television debut on the *Lew King Rangers Show*. In high school she performed in a band called *Just Us*. A few years later, she joined her two cousins band called *The Relatives*, which opened at the Sahara Hotel in Las Vegas. The band's drummer was Gary Burghoff, who played "Radar" in the television series M*A*S*H. She was voted Miss World USA 1972. From 1975 to 1979, Lynda starred in the television series *Wonder Woman*, in the role of Diana Prince, a superheroine character. In the show, she performed many of her own stunts, even hanging from a helicopter.

Actors

José Ferrer was the first Hispanic to win the Oscar for *Cyrano de Bergerac* in 1951.

Anthony Quinn won an Oscar for *Viva Zapata* in 1953, *Lust for Life* in 1957, and again for best actor in a leading role in 1958 and 1965.

Rita Moreno won the Oscar for best actress in a supporting role for the film *West Side Story* in 1962.

Mercedes Ruehl won the Oscar for best actress in a supporting role for *The Fisher King* in 1992.

Benicio Del Toro won an Oscar for his performance in *Traffic* in 2000. He was nominated again for *21 Grams* in 2003, but did not win.

Javier Bardem won an Oscar for best performance in *Traffic* in 2000.

Penélope Cruz won an Oscar for best performance in *Vicky Cristina Barcelona* in 2009.

Lupita Nyong'o won an Oscar in *12 Years a Slave* in 2013.

OTHERS, NOT ACTORS:

Alfonso Cuarón won an Oscar for Best Achievement in Directing and Best Achievements in Film Editing for the movie *Gravity* in 2014.

Alejandro González Iñárritu won an Oscar for *Birdman* in 2015. He also won an Oscar for Best Director in *The Revenant* in 2016.

Emmanuel Lubizki won an Oscar for Best Cinematography in *The Revenant* in 2016.

Gabriel Osorio and producer **Patricio "Pato" Escala** won an Oscar for Best Animated Short film in *Bear Story* in 2016.

Jonas Rivera won an Oscar for Best Animated Feature for *Inside Out* in 2016.

Humanities

The history of Hispanics in the Humanities is the heart of many subjects, telling us of our great history and culture. It preserves the knowledge of great accomplishments of others from our past, present, and future. Studying the Humanities has helped us understand our beginnings. Reading about Hispanic history and culture gives us the knowledge and insight to see the past and what the future holds for us all, with a greater understanding and appreciation for others who have gone before us, for their successes and adventures.

When the word Hispanic or Latino is used, it does not only refer to one nationality or one culture, but a great diversity of people from all over the world of different races and colors, including Spain and Latin American countries. They can be from European, Native American, Indigenous or African decent with cultural ties to Mexico, the Caribbean, Central America, South America and many other countries.

John James Audubon

John James Audubon (1785-1851), born Jean-Jacques Audubon, was French-American. He was born in Les Cayes, Santo-Domingo (now Haiti) on his father's sugar plantation. He became an ornithologist, naturalist, and painter. At a very early age he began drawing birds, and in time he became America's most well-known artist of birds in North America. Audubon decided to publish a collection of his paintings in a book, *The Birds of America*. He also created a Nature Museum. In his career he identified many new birds, painted them and recorded their behavior. In 1826, he took his collection of bird paintings to England and Scotland to display his art works and to educate the people about the finding of different birds of America. The English and Scottish people enjoyed what they saw and gave him the nickname "The American Woodsman." A portrait of John James Audubon hangs in the White House.

Stamp issued in 1960

Stamp issued in 1963

Stamp issued in 1967

Stamp issued in 1967

Stamp issued in 1998

Stamp issued in 2002

Palace of Governors

One of the oldest public buildings in the United States is an adobe building, the Palace of Governors in Santa Fe, New Mexico. The city of Santa Fe (City of Holy Faith) was founded in 1607. The Spanish, Mexicans, and Indian settlers built the Palace of Governors in 1610. The first Governor was Don Juan de Oñate, and the second was Don Pedro de Peralta.

Stamp issued in 1960

The Palace of Governors served as the seat of the government of the Spanish colonies of New Mexico, Texas, Arizona, Utah, Colorado, Nevada and California. The government of New Mexico was located at this site from 1610 until 1901. During those years, the flags of Spain, Mexico, the Confederacy and the United States flew over this historic building. In 1960, the Palace of Governors was designated as a Registered National Historic Landmark, and an American Treasure in 1999. The building is now a museum.

Mexican Independence

Miguel Hidalgo y Costilla (1753-1811), was a Mexican Roman Catholic priest and one of several leaders of the Mexican War of Independence. On September 16, 1810, Father Hidalgo made a decision that led to Mexico's struggle for independence from Spain. He heard that the Spanish had ordered his arrest, so he rang the church bell to call the people together. When the people arrived, Father Hidalgo rallied them to fight against the Spaniards. He gave a speech that is now called *Grito de Dolores* (Cry of Dolores). In it he said, *"Viva México y Viva la Independencia!"* Everyone fought including the Criollos (wealthy Mexicans of Spanish decent) and Mestizos (children of Spanish and Indian decent). They fought with clubs, knives, rocks, and whatever they could fight with all the way to Mexico City. Mexican resistance and struggle for independence began with the Spanish Conquest of the Aztec Empire. Father Hidalgo was captured and executed in 1811.

Stamp issued in 1960

International Red Cross Flag and Cuban Refugees

Cubans began migrating from Cuba to the United States to avoid the communist takeover of power by Fidel Castro. In the first two years, over 50,000 Cubans left Cuba to live in the U.S. There were three different times that the U.S. allowed Cubans to enter this country, and all three times it was under a temporary exile status, since later they were to return home to Cuba. The first was from 1959-1962, prior to the Bay of Pigs Invasion. In 1965, Cubans were allowed to enter the country, and in 1980 the third migration occurred. All the Cubans were welcomed. That year President Lyndon Johnson said, "I declare... to the people of Cuba that those who seek refuge here in America will find it." This stamp commemorated the humanitarian organization of the International Red Cross and their participation of the Cuban prisoner exchange.

Stamp issued in 1963

Alliance for Progress

The Alliance for Progress (Alianza para el Progreso) was established by the United States to aid and improve relations with the Latin American countries. President John F. Kennedy established it in 1961. After World War II, the Latin American countries that supported the U.S. in their wars felt they should receive economic assistance for helping the U.S. This program was to assist those in poverty and social inequality, and provide military and police assistance to prevent a communist takeover. The Organization of American States was disbanded in 1973.

Stamp issued in 1960

International Year of the Child

The Declaration of the Rights of the Child was adopted in an extended form by the United Nations in 1959. It was first drafted by Eglantyne Jebb and adopted by the League of Nations in 1924. It began with the work of Charles Dickens, Bramwell Booth and Beatrice Webb and others. They all wanted better standards, protection, education, health and welfare for all children. The International Year of the Child is celebrated all over the world to promote the rights and care of all children. It was designed to bring attention to all children. In 1979, an animated short film was produced called *Every Child*, which is about children that nobody wanted. Its message was to show the world that every child is somebody. The same year, on its 20th anniversary, the United Nations included an observance for children around the world. With the effort of many supporters, in 1989 it became the Convention of the Rights of the Child.

Stamp issued in 1979

Hispanic Americans - A Proud Heritage

Hispanic Americans, men and women, have always supported the United States. They have served the country at home and overseas with valor on the battlefield for more than four centuries. From the Civil War to the present, sixty-one Hispanic Americans have been awarded the highest military decoration of this nation, The Congressional Medal of Honor. Hispanic men and women have also made their contribution to the arts, sciences, music, sports, philosophy and in space. Pictured on this stamp are Hispanic men and women in military uniforms from each branch of the military. In the background of this stamp, a Hispanic young boy and girl can be seen pictured as future military leaders. The number of Hispanic men and women who laid the footprints for others to follow is endless.

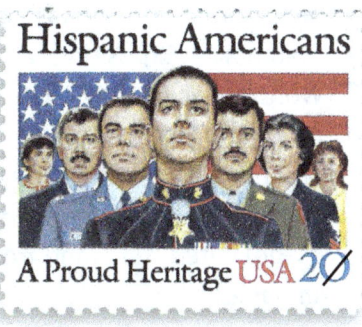

Stamp issued in 1984

Columbian Doll

The Columbian Doll was named for the Columbian Exposition at the Chicago World's Fair in 1893. The fair was held to celebrate the 400th anniversary of Christopher Columbus's arrival in the New World in 1492. The Columbian Doll traveled across the United States and around the world as *Ambassador of Goodwill*, and received the Diploma of Merit. The Columbian Doll's first trip was to Philadelphia for the benefit of children's charities. After many years of touring the U.S. and the world, the Columbian Doll was returned to Boston with collections of many newspaper clippings, and a daily log of her adventures. The Columbian Doll is at the Wenham Museum in Wenham, Massachusetts.

Stamp issued in 1997

Padre Félix Varela - Social Reformer

Padre Félix Varela Morales (1788-1853), was a Cuban Catholic priest. He was a Professor of Philosophy at the San Carlos and San Ambrosio Seminary of Havana, Cuba. A brilliant educator, he started teaching the poor to read and write. In the 1820s, Padre Varela began to help the minorities in New York City, and founded nurseries and orphanages for children of the poor. He also founded the first two Spanish Newspapers in the United States: *El Habanero* (The Native) and *El Mensajero Semanal* (The Weekly Messenger). In 1837, Father Varela was named Vicar General of the New York Diocese of the Roman Catholic Church.

Stamp issued in 1997

Desegregating Public Schools

In 1954, Brown v. Board of Education of Topeka, Kansas became a landmark decision of the U.S. Supreme Court. From 1951 to 1954, thirteen parents of twenty minority children took the school board of Topeka to court. There were separate schools for minority children, and the purpose of this lawsuit was to reverse the policy of racial segregation of minority children. These words were used in the decision, "We conclude that in the field of public education the doctrine of 'separate but equal' has no place. Separate educational facilities are inherently unequal…" With these words the court outlawed racial segregation.

Stamp issued in 1999

Cinco de Mayo

Cinco de Mayo (Fifth of May) is a holiday to celebrate Mexico's victory over the French during the Battle of Puebla on May 5, 1862. Benito Juárez was Mexico's President, the country was in ruins after the Mexican–American War, and Mexico was heading toward bankruptcy. France, Britain and Spain demanded reimbursement from Mexico for assisting in the war. In time, Spain and Britain withdrew their demands but France did not. In 1862, the Mexican Army of 4,000 soldiers led by Texas-born General Ignacio Zaragoza Seguin, led the battle that eventually gained their independence from France in 1867. This was a big victory over the French Army of 8,000 soldiers at the Battle of Puebla. This victory over the French Army was a big morale booster for the Mexican Army and to the people of Mexico and Latinos in California.

Stamp issued in 1998

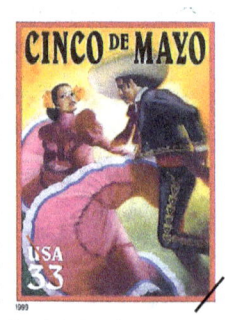

Stamp issued in 1999

California was the first to celebrate *Cinco de Mayo* in the United States. It then expanded across America among people of Mexican American heritage.

Artist for the *Cinco de Mayo* stamp is Robert Rodriguez.

Frida Kahlo

Frida Kahlo de Rivera (1907-1954), was a Mexican artist who mainly painted portraits and self-portraits. She was born Magdalena Carmen Frida Kahlo y Calderón. She was born and died in Mexico City. Her paintings are part of the pride of Mexico's national movement called *Mexicanidad*, a romantic nationalism that emerged in the aftermath of the Revolution. As a teenager Kahlo was in a traffic accident which affected her health for the rest of her life. In 1928 she married muralist Diego Rivera. Since the mid-1970s, she has been a role model for women in the feminist communities. Frida, said of herself, "I was born a painter, I paint myself because I am so often alone, and because I am the subject I know best." Frida painted some 200 paintings and drawings, 55 of which are self-portraits. Because of Frida, artists in the United States and Mexico were influenced to begin painting.

Stamp issued in 1998

Cesar E. Chavez

Stamp issued in 2003

Cesar Estrada Chavez (1927-1993), was born in the Gila River Valley near Yuma, Arizona. He began working as a farm worker at the early age of 10. At the age of 17, he joined the U.S. Navy for two years and served in the Western Pacific. After his service with the Navy he returned home and again began working the fields with his family. As a farm worker he knew in his heart he had to help other workers gain their human rights, fair wages, medical coverage, pension benefits and other rights and protections. He, along labor organizer Dolores Huerta, established the National Farm Workers Association in 1962. Later, the name was changed to United Farm Workers Union (UFW). His motto became *Sí, se puede* ("Yes, it can be done" or "Yes we can"). He was the UFW's president and served until his death in 1993. In 1994, President Clinton posthumously awarded Chavez the Presidential Medal of Freedom. In 2012, President Barack Obama said of him, "No one seemed to care about the invisible farm workers who picked the nation's food...but Cesar cared..." Obama signed a Presidential Proclamation creating the Cesar E. Chavez National Monument in Kern County, California. It became the 398th Monument in the National Park Service. After his death in 1993, many parks, cultural centers, libraries, schools and streets across America have been named after him in his honor.

Artist for the Cesar E. Chavez stamp is Robert Rodriguez.

Jaime Escalante

Jaime Escalante (1930-2010), born Jaime Alfonso Escalante Gutiérrez, was an educator from La Paz, Bolivia. Escalante taught math and physics for twelve years in Bolivia before coming to the United States. In the U.S. he began teaching calculus at Garfield High School in East Los Angeles, California to students that other teachers had given up on. With Escalante teaching them, all the students passed the Advanced Placement (AP) test. In 1988, a book about him was published, *Escalante: The Best Teacher in America*. A movie in which Escalante was the math teacher titled *Stand and Deliver* was released in 1988. In 1993, an asteroid discovered 10 years earlier at the Lowell Observatory in Flagstaff, Arizona was named after him, 5095 Escalante.

Stamp issued in 2016

Ruben Salazar

Ruben Salazar (1928-1970), was born in Ciudad Juarez, Chihuahua Mexico. He was a journalist for the *Los Angeles Times* and a spokesman for Latinos. He received a degree in journalism at Texas Western College. He served two years in the United States Army. After his military service he worked as a journalist for El Paso Herald-Post. He also was a foreign correspondent and in his early years he reported from Vietnam, and at one time was captured by terrorists in Panama. He had concerns about racism and abuse of Latinos by police in the U.S. He reported during the National Chicano Moratorium March against the Vietnam War. Salazar died during the National Chicano Moratorium March against the Vietnam War on August 29, 1970.

Mendez v. Westminster

Stamp issued in 2007

In 1946, five Mexican-American fathers: Gonzalo Mendez, Thomas Estrada, William Guzman, Frank Palomino and Lorenzo Ramirez, successfully challenged school segregation in the U.S. District Court in Los Angeles. At that time California law provided for segregation of students. The fathers claimed that their children, along with 5,000 other children of Mexican-American ancestry, African-Americans and Japanese-Americans, were victims of discrimination by forcing them to attend separate schools in the Westminster, Garden Grove, Santa Ana, and El Modena school districts. The NAACP joined with them in support of the case. The plaintiffs won the case. The courts found that segregation in schools is unconstitutional because it did not provide equal protection for their children.

The artist for *Mendez V. Westminster* is Rafael Lopez. He has other stamps: *Latin Music Legends* and *Let's Dance Merengue*.

Severo Ochoa An American Scientist

Severo Ochoa, born Severo Ochoa de Albornoz (1905-1993), was a biochemist born in Asturias, Spain. He attended the University of Madrid, where he received his M.D. in 1929. In 1942, he was appointed Research Associate in Medicine at New York University and became Assistant Professor of Biochemistry in 1945. In 1956, he became a United States citizen. He was professor of Pharmacology in 1946, and in 1959, he received the Nobel Prize in Physiology and Medicine. Ochoa was the Professor and Chair of Biochemistry at New York University Langone Medical Center from 1954 to 1974. He spent 35 years at the New York University School of Medicine.

Stamp issued in 2011

Felipe Rojas-Lombardi

Felipe Rojas-Lombardi (1945-1991), was a Master Chef born in Lima, Peru. At a very young age Felipe enjoyed cooking and wanted to become a chef. When Felipe became older, he attended law school in Peru, but he still wanted to become a chef. In 1967, he moved from Lima, Peru to New York City to become a chef and attended the Greenwich Village Cooking School. Felipe brought South American, Spanish, and Latin cooking to America. In 1976, he was named America's Bicentennial Chef. In the same year he also became a United States citizen. He was on the PBS TV series called *New York's Master Chefs*. He also published two books, *The Art of South American Cooking*, and *Soup, Beautiful Soup*.

Stamp issued in 2014

HUMANITIES

Father Junípero Serra

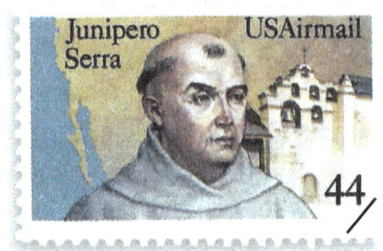

Stamp issued in 1985

Father Junípero Serra (1713-1784), born Miguel José Serra Ferrer, was a Roman Catholic Spanish Franciscan priest. He was born in a farming village in Petra, Island of Majorca, Spain. At the age of 16 he entered the Franciscan Order, taking the name Junípero in honor of Saint Juniper. He founded his first Mission in Baja California and then another in Alta (upper) California in the Province of Las Californias, New Spain. He, along with the Native Americans and Mexicans, began growing oranges, lemons, olives, figs and grapes. He founded the first nine of 21 Missions in California, from San Diego to San Francisco, and baptized over 6,000 Native Americans and Mexicans to Christianity. The Juniper Serra Peak in Santa Lucia, California is named in his honor.

Space Achievements

Stamps issued in 1981

At a very early age, many Hispanic children only dreamed of going into space. Many would watch television to learn about the Space Shuttle Program of the National Aeronautics and Space Administration (NASA), and said to themselves, "I want to go into space." Some of them did. Because of their dreams, hard work, and education they achieved their goals and became astronauts. Below is a list of the Hispanic men and women astronauts.

Arnaldo Tamayo Méndez, first Cuban to fly in space.

Rodolfo Neri Vela, first Mexican to fly in space.

Franklin Chang Díaz, first Costa Rican in space.

Sidney M. Gutierrez, first Mexican-American in space.

Ellen Ochoa, first and only Mexican-American woman in space, and second female director of NASA's Johnson Space Center.

Michael López-Alegría, first Spanish-American in space.

Carlos I. Noriega, first Peruvian in space.

Pedro Duque, from Spain.

John D. Olivas, from USA.

George D. Zamka, from USA.

Joseph M. Acaba, from USA.

José Hernández, from USA.

Serena M. Auñón, from Cuba. Candidate.

José López Falcón, from Cuba. Backup.

Ricardo Peralta y Fabi, from Mexico. Their mission was cancelled after Challenger disaster.

Fernando Caldeiro, from Argentina. Candidate.

Christopher Loria, from USA. Candidate.

States

There are eight states in America that were given Spanish or Native American names. The eight states are: Arizona, California, Colorado, Florida, Montana, Nevada, New Mexico and Texas. Over 2,000 cities across America have Hispanic names: Los Angeles, San Diego, Las Cruces, El Paso and Corpus Christi, just to name a few. The city named Galveston, Texas was named for General Bernardo de Gálvez, a Spanish-American General in the American Revolution.

ARIZONA

The name Arizona comes from the Spanish word arizuma, which is an Aztec word meaning silver-bearing. For the Pima Native Americans, Arizona was known as arizonac, meaning little spring place. Arizona became the 48th U.S. state on February 14, 1912. Many explorers crossed Arizona, including Marcos de Niza, a Spanish missionary and Franciscan friar who explored Arizona in 1539. Father Kino, born Eusebius Chinus, an Italian missionary, geographer, and cartographer, was also one of the early explorers of Arizona. Arizona is the home of the Navajo Nation, Hopi Tribe, Tohono O'odham, Apache Tribe and many more Native American people. Many Hispanic and Native American men and women built irrigation canals for farming and ranching. Many Anglos began migrating into Arizona after the Civil War, moving into Hispanic and Native American communities, and some of the towns' names were changed: Rio Salado became Tempe; Pueblo Viejo became Solomonville, later changed to Solomon.

Arizona is home to three Congressional Medal of Honor recipients: Silvestre S. Herrera, José Francisco Jimenez and Jay R. Vargas.

Arizona Statehood

Arizona was at different times ruled by Spain, Mexico, and the United States. For 20 years, Arizona fought with the U.S. Congress to become a state. At one time Congress wanted to make Arizona and New Mexico one state, but Arizona and New Mexico both disagreed. Arizona became the 48th state on February 14, 1912.

Arizona is the home of the Grand Canyon National Park. A member of the Francisco Vázquez de Coronado expedition, Captain García López de Cárdenas, was the first to see the Grand Canyon. The canyon is one of the Seven Natural Wonders of the World, and also one of the first National Parks in the United States.

Stamp issued in 1962

Several Native American tribes have lived throughout time in the Grand Canyon. One quarter of Arizona is federal land and home of the Navajo Nation, Hopi Tribe, Tohono O'odham, Apache Tribe, Yaqui natives and many more.

San Xavier del Bac Mission

San Xavier del Bac Mission is a Spanish Catholic mission located on the Tohono O'odham San Xavier Indian Reservation, near Tucson, Arizona. The mission is known as "White Dove of the Desert." It is also known as the "place where water appears," because there once was a natural spring.

Stamp issued in 1971

Father Eusebio Kino founded the mission in 1692 to serve the local Papago tribe. Today's renovated building, which is part Moorish and Byzantine, has a domed roof and is made of adobe bricks, with carved saints and two lions. The lions represent Castile and are often decorated with white satin bow ties.

USS Arizona Memorial

The USS Arizona was docked at Pearl Harbor in Honolulu, Hawaii, when the Japanese surprised the United States with the air attack on the morning of December 7, 1941. A total of 1,177 sailors and marines were killed, and many are entombed in their ships. In Phoenix, Arizona, the 15-inch gun, two of the masts and the anchor of the USS Arizona are displayed on the grounds in front of the Arizona State Capitol. There were many Hispanics who perished aboard the USS Arizona and other ships.

Stamp issued in 2014

Flying off the USS Enterprise on December 7 was Ensign Pilot Manuel "Manny" Gonzalez, the first American casualty at Pearl Harbor. As he was scouting the area, it is believed that he flew into the Japanese aircraft as they were headed to Pearl Harbor near the Island of Oahu. Ensign Gonzalez and his aircraft were never located.

Aboard the USS Nevada was Marine PFC Richard I. Trujillo. He was the first Hispanic marine killed in World War II at Pearl Harbor.

Rudy Martinez, Navy 3rd Class, was the first sailor killed aboard the USS Utah during the attack at Pearl Harbor. The American Legion Post 624 in Mansfield, Texas, is named in his honor, The Rudolph M. Martinez American Legion Post 624.

CALIFORNIA "CALIFIA"

The State of California, "Califia," was named for the warrior queen "Califia, The Empress of California." Queen Califia was a Black queen living in a kingdom of women. The early Spaniards had heard about the legend of Califia and named the region after her, then changed it to California. In 1926, a portrait of Queen Califia was placed in the Room of Dons at the Mark Hopkins Hotel in San Francisco. The novel *Las Sergas de Esplandián* (The Adventures of Esplandián) was written about her in 1500 by Garci Rodríguez de Montalvo. In the U.S. history books there is no mention of Califia.

The capital of California is Sacramento, its nickname is the Golden State and the motto is Eureka, a Greek word that means "I have found it." California became a United States Territory in 1769, and the 31st U.S. state on September 9, 1850. When the Spanish first explored the California Pacific Coast they believed that it was an island. Portuguese navigator Juan Rodriguez Cabrillo sighted California in 1542, 50 years after Christopher Columbus arrived to the New World. The first Spanish mission was Mission Basilica San Diego de Alcalá, established in 1769.

Yosemite National Park El Capitán

Yosemite National Park is located in the Sierra Nevada Mountains in California, and covers 747,956 acres of land. In 1984 it became a World Heritage Site. It has granite cliffs, waterfalls, streams and giant sequoia trees, some of which are over 3,000 years old. The Paiute, Miwok and Mono tribes lived in the area before the first explorers arrived. Native Americans called the Ahwahneechee lived in the Yosemite Valley for thousands of years. Their chief was Chief Tenaya. Dr. Lafayette Bunnell named the area Yosemite, believing it to be the name of the local tribe living there. The Spanish named a distinctive high mountain *El Capitán* (The Captain). Yosemite became a National Park October 1, 1890.

Stamp issued in 1932

Carmel Mission Belfry

Carmel Mission, a Roman Catholic mission church, was named after San Carlos Borroméo del Río Carmelo, a 16th Century Italian cardinal. The Carmel Mission is one of California's heritage sites, it is on the National Register of Historic Places and a United States National Historic Landmark. Carmel Mission was the second of 21 missions built from San Diego to San Francisco. It was located near the native village of Tamo, and was the site of the first Christian confirmation of a native in Alta (Upper) California.

Stamp issued in 1969

Alta California

In 1777, Spain created the first settlement in Alta (Upper) California, which is now called San José (El Pueblo de San José de Guadalupe). This settlement in Alta California had a big influence on the West Coast and the entire United States. The territory of Viceroyalty (Spanish overseas territories) of Alta California was the center for all social and administrative activities created by the Spanish in the 15th Century of New Spain, later a territory of Mexico. After the Mexican–American War, Alta California became a territory of the State of California.

Stamp issued in 1977

California Pacific International Exposition

The first California Pacific International Exposition was held in San Diego, California, in Balboa Park from May 29 to November 11, 1935. Then again from February 12 to September 9, 1936. The exposition celebrated the 400th anniversary of Coronado's discovery of the Pacific Southwest. It included exhibits featuring science, culture, industry and the arts. Other attractions included a recreation of an 1849 mining town called *Gold Gulch*. Not only was there a stamp issued at this time, but also the government released a commemorative silver half dollar. Today the coin is known as the "San Diego Half." Both the stamp and the silver half dollar were released at the same time.

Stamp issued in 1935

COLORADO

The capital of Colorado is Denver. Colorado is nicknamed the Centennial State because it became a state in the centennial year of the United States Declaration of Independence. It was admitted to the Union on August 1, 1876, and became the 38th state. Its motto is *Nil Sine Numine*, Latin words meaning "Nothing without the Deity." The name Colorado was given by the Spanish explorers because of the red sandstone soil. The U.S. took control of Colorado in 1848 with the Treaty of Guadalupe that ended the Mexican-American War (1846-1848).

Kenneth Lee Salazar, a United States Senator from 2005-2009, served as the 50th United States Secretary of the Interior in the Administration of President Obama from 2009-2013. His older brother, John Salazar, was also a former congressman. The Salazar family has been in Colorado since the 16th Century, when Colorado was still part of New Spain. They were the first family to settle in the San Luis Valley and are still there today.

Mesa Verde, Colorado

In Mesa Verde, Colorado, there are 40 ancient Native American dwellings visible in the canyon. Pueblo people lived in these man-made dwellings over 1000 years ago. Franciscan priests and explorers Francisco Atanasio Domínguez (Mexican) and Silvestre Vélez de Escalante (Spanish), were travelling from Santa Fe, New Mexico to California in 1776. They saw the adobe and stone structures, and gave them the name Mesa Verde (Spanish for green table). They never explored the structures, but they did record their findings in 1776. In 1888, while gathering their herd of cattle, two *vaqueros* (cowboys) on horseback rode into the canyon and noticed the adobe structures. In their search of the structures the *vaqueros* noticed pottery, woven baskets and different types of tools that had been there for hundreds of years. In 1978, Mesa Verde was declared a World Heritage Site. Today, the Mesa Verde National Park protects over 5000 archeological sites.

Stamp issued in 1934

Colorado Capitol and Mount Holy Cross

This stamp shows the Colorado State Capitol, a cowboy, and on the left side Mount Holy Cross is seen. For many years there was a legend told about Mount Holy Cross by Spanish explorers in the 1700s. As snow filled the mountain, the pattern of snow showed a cross. In the winter two Spanish priests who were lost on their way to New Mexico got stranded in a freezing blizzard. Then they noticed what looked like a cross on the hillside of the mountain. Was the sighting of the cross a sign or a vision of hope to move on? This vision of the cross encouraged the priests, and they eventually survived. In 1873, F.V. Hayden, a geographer, was in search of the "great white cross." He wanted to take a picture of the cross but could not locate it. Hayden met the Ute Chief Ouray, who knew the location of the cross and took Hayden and his crew to view it. A picture of Mount Holy Cross was published in newspapers across America. The mount was named for the large cross-shaped feature on its northeast face.

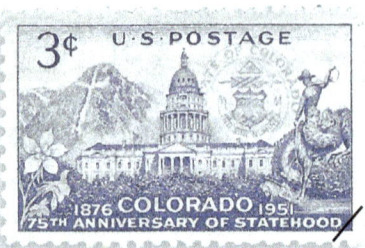

Stamp issued in 1951

FLORIDA

In 1513, Juan Ponce de León, was the first known Spanish European navigator to set foot in Florida and claim the new land for Spain. Ponce de León sailed along the Florida east coast, and landing in the new land named it "La Florida," the Place of Flowers. In time, the name of the place where some historians believe he landed changed to Saint Augustine. While sailing the coast, he also named the area Cape Canaveral, meaning Cape of Currents, for the rough currents in that location. In 1819, the Florida territory came into United States' control with the Florida Purchase Treaty between Spain and the U.S. In 1845, Florida became the 27th state, and Tallahassee became the Capital.

Other early Spanish explorers who also came to Florida were Pánfilo de Narváez in 1528, Hernando de Soto in 1539, and Pedro Menéndez de Avilés in 1565.

La Florida

The Capital of Florida is Tallahassee, and the state is nicknamed the Sunshine State. Their motto was *E Pluribus Unum*, Latin words meaning "One out of many," but in 1956 it was changed to "In God We Trust." Spanish explorer Juan Ponce de León departed in March 4, 1513 from Puerto Rico, and on April 2, 1513 he sighted the Florida Peninsula. He went ashore on Florida's East Coast during the Spanish Easter feast Pascua Florida, which means flowery festival or feast of flowers, but it refers to the Easter season (The Passion of the Christ). Ponce de León named the new land *La Pascua de la Florida*. Florida became a United States territory in 1822. In 1845, Florida was admitted to the Union, making it the 27th State.

Stamps issued in 2013

Florida Statehood

Florida was a United States territory from 1822 to 1845. In 1845, Florida became the 27th State. The state flag of Florida was adopted in 1900. The flag is on a white field with a red X and the state seal. Juan Ponce de León (1474-1521), a Spanish explorer, reached Florida in 1513. Claiming the region for Spain, he named the new land "La Pascua de la Florida," in honor of the "Pascua Florida," a Spanish Easter feast. In his explorations he was searching for the "Fountain of Youth," but never found it. In 1521, Ponce de León returned to Florida to start colonizing that new land.

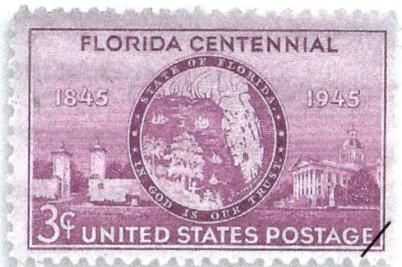

Stamp issued in 1945

Settlement of Florida

Florida became the 27th U.S. state in 1845. The Spanish were the first Europeans to settle in the New World, then the French, and then the English. Spanish Admiral Don Pedro Menéndez de Avilés founded Saint Augustine in 1565, naming the location in honor of the saint whose feast day was on the day the settlement was established. This stamp was issued to mark the 400th anniversary of the founding of Saint Augustine. At the same time, Spain also released an almost identical stamp. Over 14,000 years ago, Native Americans were the first people in Florida.

Stamp issued in 1965

MONTANA

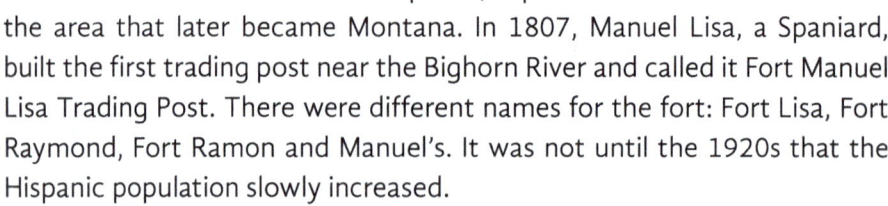

Hispanic explorers were in Montana many years before it was a state. The explorers, trappers and *vaqueros* (cowboys) were the first non-natives to enter the area of what is now called Montana. In 1743, Louis-Joseph Gaultier de *La Vérendrye*, a French Canadian fur trader and explorer, explored the area that later became Montana. In 1807, Manuel Lisa, a Spaniard, built the first trading post near the Bighorn River and called it Fort Manuel Lisa Trading Post. There were different names for the fort: Fort Lisa, Fort Raymond, Fort Ramon and Manuel's. It was not until the 1920s that the Hispanic population slowly increased.

"Treasure State"

Montana's capital is Helena. It is nicknamed the "Treasure State" or "Big Sky Country." Montana's motto is *Oro y Plata*, meaning "Gold and Silver." The name Montana comes from the Spanish word *montaña*, and the Latin word *montana* means "mountain." The names of Montana and other mountainous regions of the West were given by Spanish explorers. Montana became a territory in 1803 with the Louisiana Purchase, then became a United States territory on May 26, 1864, and the 41st state on November 8, 1889.

Stamp issued in 1934

Stamp issued in 1989

NEVADA

Nevada means covered in snow. The capital is Carson City. Nicknames are "Silver State" and "Sage State." Nevada's motto is "All for Our Country." Between 1540 and 1542, Spanish conquistador and explorer Francisco Vázquez de Coronado, led a failed attempt to explore the region that centuries later became the state of Nevada. A Spanish priest, Francisco Garcés, entered into the northeast part of Nevada in the 1770s. In 1804, Nevada became part of Alta California under the Spanish Empire. It became part of the U.S. when it was established as a territory in 1848 with the Treaty of Guadalupe Hidalgo between the U.S. and Mexico, and joined the Union as the 36th state on October 31, 1864.

Judge John F. Mendoza (1928-2011) was the first Hispanic from Nevada to attend Notre Dame University with a football scholarship in 1945. In 1951, Mendoza was the first Hispanic attorney to be licensed in Nevada. In 1966, he was elected and served as judge for the Clark County District until 1990. Judge Mendoza later started the first Latin American Bar Association (LABA). He served in the U.S. Army as well.

Battle Born State

Nevada became the 36th state in 1864, eight days before the presidential election of 1864 between Lincoln and McClellan. Nevada is known as the "Battle Born State," because it became a state during the American Civil War (1861-1865). Native Americans including the Paiute, Shoshone and Washoe, inhabited the land before the Spanish explorers arrived. Francisco Garcés was the first Spanish explorer to enter the area of present-day Nevada. Garcés had also explored the U.S. Southwest and Mexico, and gave the Colorado River its name. Spain claimed the land as part of Alta California until the Mexico War of Independence brought it under the control of Mexico.

Stamp issued in 1951

Stamp issued in 1964

NEW MEXICO

There were many Spanish conquistadores and friars who explored New Mexico in search of new lands and converts for Spain, among them Francisco Vázquez de Coronado, Francisco Sánchez, Agustín Rodríguez, Juan de Oñate, and others.

On September 21, 1595, King Philip II of Spain appointed Don Juan de Oñate (1550-1626) as the first territorial governor of New Mexico from 1598 to 1608. In 1778, Juan Bautista de Anza (1736-1788) became Governor of New Mexico for the Spanish Empire. New Mexico became a United States territory in 1853. This same year, José Manuel Gallegos was elected as a Democrat to the 33rd U.S. Congress of the Territory of New Mexico.

The colors of the state's flag are red and yellow for the colors of the Spanish flag. The Red Sun in the center is a symbol of the Zia Native Americans. New Mexico, also known as the "Land of Enchantment," became the 47th state on January 6, 1912.

Governor Susana Martinez became the first Latina governor of New Mexico in 2011, and the first Latina governor in the U.S.

New Mexico, Land of Enchantment

New Mexico's capital is Santa Fe, its nickname is the Land of Enchantment, and motto is *Crescit Eundo*, a phrase that in Latin means "Grows as it goes."

Stamp issued in 1962

Francisco Vázquez de Coronado, led an expedition from Mexico from 1540 to 1542 to explore and attempt to find the Seven Cities of Cibola, a legend told by Álvar Núñez Cabeza de Vaca about seven cities of gold that could be found throughout the pueblos of the New Mexico Territory. In 1610, the "Palace of the Governors" was built in Santa Fe. It is one of the oldest public buildings in the United States, and was the seat of the government from 1610 until 1901. With the Treaty of Guadalupe Hidalgo, New Mexico came under the control of the U.S., and then was designated as a territory in 1853 as part of the Gadsden Purchase.

Rio Grande Blankets

Stamps issued in 2005

The Rio Grande Blankets were woven by Hispanics who lived in the Rio Grande Valley dating back many centuries and in time became an important part of the local economy. The blankets were also in great demand as trading items. They were a major export item to Mexico. Later, the blankets were known as the Rio Grande Blankets of New Mexico. The wool came from the Navajo-Churro sheep, a breed that originated with the Spanish-Churra sheep brought over by the Spaniards in the Coronado Expedition in 1540. The families who raised the sheep cut the wool to produce yarn for weaving the blankets. All blankets were handmade, and were used to protect the settlers from the cold winter nights. In time, American scholars and art collectors began to appreciate the blankets, and now many of them are preserved and placed in museums across America.

TEXAS

Texas began with the Spanish explorers in 1519. At that time, there had been many Native American tribes in Texas for thousands of years. The first to map the Texas coastline was Alonso Álvarez de Pineda in 1519. In 1718, Spanish missionaries were the first to settle in San Antonio.

From 1519 to 1848 five different countries claimed Texas: France, Spain, Mexico, The Republic of Texas, and finally the United States. In 1845, Texas became the 28th U.S. state. The name Texas came from the Caddo Nation word *tejas*, meaning "friend" or "allies." It later became the state motto: Friendship.

Marcelino Serna (1896-1992), was an undocumented Mexican who emigrated from Mexico to El Paso, Texas. Serna became the most decorated soldier from Texas in World War I and the first Latino to be awarded the Distinguished Service Cross, the second highest military award.

"Lone Star State"

The capital of Texas is Austin, its nickname is the "Lone Star State," and its motto is *Friendship*. In 1519, the first Spanish conquistadors entered what is now Texas. A famous fight for Texas independence was the Battle of the Alamo. It took place in San Antonio on March 6, 1836, following a 13-day siege. The Caddo Nation tribe gave Texas its name. In Spanish the word *tejas*, means "friends." *Tejas* then became Texas. Texas was admitted in the Union on December 29, 1845. It has one star on its flag meaning "The Lone Star State."

The Statehood of Texas began in 1845. After the Battle of Gonzales in 1835, this was the beginning of the Texas War of Independence from Mexico. Stephen F. Austin was the founder of the Texas Rangers in 1823. The first known Texas Ranger was Francisco Acosta (1838), and his commander was Lewis Sanchez. José Félix Trespalacios served as the Governor of *Tejas* (Texas) from 1831 to 1833. He approved the Texas Rangers.

Stamp issued in 1945

Stamp issued in 1986

The Alamo

The Alamo (Mission of San Antonio de Valero) was the home of the missionaries and the Native American Nations Payaya, Sama, Pachaque and others for 70 years. The Alamo represents the fighting spirit of Texans and Tejanos who fought in the mission for 13 days for their independence from Mexico during the Texas Revolution. Many men died defending the Alamo. Texans William B. Travis, James Bowie, Davy Crockett; and Tejanos Juan Abamillo, Juan A. Badillo, Carlos Espalier, José Gregorio Esparza, Antonio Fuentes, José Maria Guerrero, Damacio Jiménez, Toribio Losoya and Andrés Nava were inside the Alamo to fight against Santa Anna's army, and for Texas. After the battle, there were only twelve survivors. The wives and children of the men fighting Santa Anna's army were all released without harm.

Stamp issued in 1936

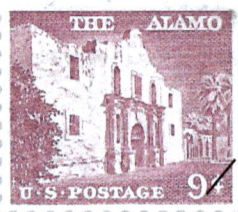

Stamp issued in 1956

HemisFair '68

In 1968, the World Fair exhibition was held in San Antonio, Texas. Texas held its 250th Anniversary celebration with the opening of the Hemisfair '68. The exhibition also celebrated the 250th anniversary of San Antonio, which was founded in 1718. San Antonio was chosen for the celebration for having a very large cultural mix of Hispanic heritage. The theme of the World Fair was called the "Confluence of Civilizations in the Americas." Hemisfair '68 celebrated the history of the Old World to the coming of the New World. This was the first World Fair held in the U.S. Southwest. In the grand Texas tradition, no small party would do.

Stamp issued in 1968

Political

Hispanic politicians in America, from both Democrat and Republican parties, have all worked for their constituency for many years for equal civil rights. As the Hispanic population increases, the number of Hispanics in politics also grows. Listed below are a few past and present politicians who have served in government.

Charles Dominique Joseph Bouligny (1773-1833), a Spanish—American, U.S. Senator from Louisiana from 1824-1829.

José Antonio Romualdo Pacheco (1831-1899), a Mexican-American politician. Pacheco had a 39-year career in politics as California State Senator, 12th Governor of California, and three terms in the U.S. House of Representatives. Pacheco was also the state's first governor to be born in California before statehood.

Octaviano Ambrosio Larrazolo (1859-1930), a Mexican-American Republican politician. He was the 4th Governor of New Mexico from 1928-1929, and a United States Senator. He was the first Hispanic United States Senator of Mexican-American heritage.

Joseph Manuel Montoya (1915-1978), a Mexican-American U.S. Senator for New Mexico from 1964 to 1977.

Dennis Chavez (1888-1962), a Mexican—American United States Senator for New Mexico for 32 years.

Susana Martinez, the first Mexican-American woman who in 2011 became the 31st Governor of New Mexico, and the first Latina Governor in the United States.

Sonia Sotomayor, a Puerto Rican-American from New York, has been a Justice of the U.S. Supreme Court since 2009. Sotomayor is the first Latina and the third woman to be appointed to the Supreme Court.

Dennis Chavez

Stamp issued in 1991

Dennis Chavez (1888-1962), was a Mexican-American politician. As a United States Senator, Chavez fought for the human rights of Hispanics and Native Americans in his home state. He served in the U.S. House of Representatives from 1931-1935, and then in the U.S. Senate for 27 years, from 1935 to 1962. Chavez was accepted at Georgetown University Law School and received his Law degree in 1920. He returned to Albuquerque to open his first law office. In 1922, he was elected to the State House of Representatives in New Mexico. In 1937, he introduced the first of many bills to protect Native land, citizenship and voting rights for all. He believed in equal civil rights for everyone. While other politicians avoided the subject of discrimination against Hispanics and Native Americans, Senator Chavez was not afraid to speak out about the issue. He was the first person of Hispanic descent to complete his term in office and was reelected to a full term in the U.S. Senate.

Simón Bolívar

Simón Bolívar, born Simón José Antonio de la Santísima Trinidad Bolívar (1783-1830), was a Venezuelan military and political leader. The South American General was known as *El Libertador* (The Liberator) in present-day nations, and he is considered one of the greatest military figures in South American history. His victories helped Bolivia (named in his honor), Colombia, Ecuador, Peru and Venezuela win independence from Spain. After France invaded Spain in 1808, he became involved with the resistance, and played a key role in South America's fight for independence. General Bolívar became President of Colombia in December 1819.

Simón Bolívar was honored in the Champion of Liberty stamp series, honoring non-Americans from their homeland.

Stamp issued in 1958

Stamp issued in 1958

José de San Martín

José de San Martín (1778-1850), born in Argentina, became a general and statesman. General de San Martín was the leader of the southern part of South America who fought for independence from the Spanish. He organized others to defeat the Spanish military, also developed the new "Army of the Andes" in Cuyo Province, and brought freedom to his native Argentina. He also won independence for Chile and Peru, which made him a national hero in both countries. The Order of the Liberator General San Martín was created in his honor; it is the highest decoration given by the Argentina government.

José de San Martín was honored in the Champion of Liberty stamp series, honoring non-Americans from their homeland.

Stamp issued in 1959

Stamp issued in 1959

Puerto Rico

Puerto Rico means rich port, the capital is San Juan, and its motto is *Joannes est nomen eius* (John is his name). Christopher Columbus named the island San Juan Bautista after the Catholic Saint John the Baptist and named the capital "Ciudad de Puerto Rico" (Puerto Rico City). Puerto Rico was a very important military post for many wars between Spain and other countries in the 16th, 17th, and 18th centuries. After the Spanish-American War, Puerto Rico became a territory of the United States in 1898. The Foraker Act of 1900 was established by the U.S., and became the Jones Act of 1917, which made Puerto Ricans citizens of the United States. In 1917, Puerto Rico was given United States citizenship, but the people of Puerto Rico could not vote in a presidential election.

La Fortaleza, Puerto Rico

La Fortaleza (The Fortress) of Puerto Rico is the official residence of the Governor of Puerto Rico. It was built in 1533. It is also known as the Palacio de Santa Catalina (Santa Catalina's Palace), and it is the oldest executive mansion of the New World. La Fortaleza was built so incoming ships could be seen in the harbor and for the purpose of defending the harbor of San Juan from invaders. La Fortaleza has been the residence of more than 170 governors and many dignitaries have visited there, including President John F. Kennedy and his wife Jacqueline, the King of Spain Juan Carlos, and Queen Juliana of the Netherlands. In 2011, U.S. President Barack Obama also visited La Fortaleza.

Stamp issued in 1937

Puerto Rico Election

In 1949, José Luis Alberto Muñoz Marín, known as Luis Muñoz Marín, became Puerto Rico's first elected governor. Before this election, the King of Spain or the President of the United States appointed the governor of Puerto Rico. As Governor, Marín started Operation Commonwealth. The goal of the program was to achieve more self-rule from the United States. Puerto Rico became a commonwealth of the United States in 1952, as a result of Marín's effort.

Stamp issued in 1949

Sila María Calderón became the first woman to be elected Governor of Puerto Rico in the 2000 election, and served as governor from 2001 to 2005.

San Juan, Puerto Rico

S an Juan, Puerto Rico, founded by Spaniard Juan Ponce de León, is the oldest foreign city to fly the American Flag. The first settlement of Puerto Rico was Caparra, and in 1508 became the first headquarters in the New World. Twenty years later, San Juan had its first university, hospital, and library. San Juan today is known as *La ciudad amurallada* (The Walled City). In 1521 it was named San Juan Bautista de Puerto Rico, in honor of John the Baptist. For the Spanish explorers this was the first layover in the New World. The first governor was Juan Ponce de León.

Stamp issued in 1971

La Cueva del Indio

L a Cueva del Indio (Cave of the Indian) is one of Puerto Rico's mysterious caves. It is located near Arecibo on Puerto Rico's north coastline. The cave is known for the engravings and drawings on the walls, which include faces, a sun, geometric shapes, animals, wedding ceremonies and ball games. The Taino Natives made many of the carvings, and these petro glyphic drawings are predated centuries before Columbus' landing in 1493. *La Cueva del Indio* came under protection in 2003 by the National Registrar of Historic Monuments.

Stamp issued in 2016

José Ferrer

José Ferrer, José Vicente Ferrer de Otero y Cintrón (1912-1992), was born in San Juan, Puerto Rico. He was an actor, theater and film director. He graduated from Princeton University in 1933. He was the first Hispanic to win an Academy Award, for his famous dance performance *Cyrano de Bergerac* in 1950. He made his Hollywood debut in *Joan of Arc* in 1948. Later he played the role of Miguel de Cervantes, and fictional character *Don Quixote* in the musical *Man of La Mancha*. He played the role in 1946 and 1953, and in film in 1950. He was the only actor to win the Oscar, the Emmy, and the Tony Award for the same character. He was also awarded the National Medal of Arts in 1985. He returned to the stage many times for a performance later in his career, and also went on many tours.

Stamp issued in 2010

The Academy Awards, nicknamed Oscar, are given to the winners at the annual American Awards ceremony honoring achievements in the movie industry. Eleven Hispanic men and women have won the Academy Awards. Of the 11, only one is on a stamp: José Ferrer.

Julia de Burgos

Julia de Burgos, born Julia Constanza de Burgos García (1914-1953), was a Puerto Rican poet, civil rights activist and a nationalist. An advocate for Puerto Rico, she served as Secretary General of the Daughters of the Freedom of the Women of the Puerto Rican Nationalist Party. She graduated from the University of Puerto Rico and became a teacher. Her first poem was published at the age of nineteen. Her best-known poem is *Río Grande de Loíza*. She is considered one of Latin America's greatest poets. *Poema para mi muerte* ("My Death Poem"), and *Yo misma fui mi ruta* ("I Was My Own Path"), are two of her well-known poems. In her words, "My childhood was all a poem in the river, and a river in the poem of my first dream." An art center was named after her. The Cultural Education Institute founded the Julia de Burgos Cultural Arts Center for Boricua Advancement (CEIBA), and The Latino Parent's Union.

Stamp issued in 2010

Sports

In every professional sport there have been Hispanic men and women players, including baseball, football, basketball, tennis, golf and other sports.

Hispanics have made a name for themselves and many are in a Hall of Fame for their respective sport and have paved the way for other Hispanics to follow. The first Hispanic to play in the Major League Baseball (MLB) in 1868 was Esteban Bellán, a Cuban-American professional player.

Baseball

Roy "Campy" Campanella (1921-1993) played baseball as a catcher in the American Negro Leagues in 1937, and also played in the Mexican League from 1942 to 1943. Campanella, Jackie Robinson and others broke the color barriers of Major League Baseball. He signed with the Brooklyn Dodgers in 1947, and in 1948 he played in his first professional game. In 1953 Campy would hit 41 homeruns.

Campanella is considered one of the greatest catchers in the history of baseball. He received the Most Valuable Player Award (MVP) in the National League three times, in 1951, 1953 and 1955. In 1950, the Philadelphia native was the first Dodgers player to hit home runs in five straight games. He was inducted into the Baseball Hall of Fame in 1969.

Roberto Enrique Walker Clemente (1934-1972), was born in San Anton, Puerto Rico, and the son of sugarcane workers. He became a great Major League Baseball player in 1955 playing right field with the Pittsburgh Pirates. He first played with the Brooklyn Dodgers, then played 18 seasons for the Pirates from 1955-1972. He was an All Star 12 times. In

1972 he hit his 3,000 major league hit, becoming the first Latino baseball player to hit 3,000 hits and 240 home runs. In 1973 he was inducted into the National Baseball Hall of Fame. Proud of his Hispanic and African-American roots, he always said, "I don't believe in color. I believe in people…my mother and father taught me never to hate, never to dislike someone because of their color."

Clemente was not just a great baseball player but also a great humanitarian. He was always trying to support the poor. He died in an airplane crash while attempting to deliver supplies to earthquake victims in Nicaragua on December 31, 1972.

Ted Williams, born Theodore Samuel Williams (1918-2002), was a professional baseball player and manager; he was known as one of the greatest baseball batters in baseball history. Ted was born in San Diego, California. Ted's mother was May Venzor, a Mexican-American from El Paso, Texas. At the age of 8, Ted's maternal uncle Saul Venzor, taught Ted how to play baseball. Ted played professional baseball for 19 years for the Boston Red Sox.

In 1942, Ted joined the U.S. Navy Reserve and was commissioned as a Second Lieutenant in the U.S. Marine Corps, as a Naval Aviator fighter pilot in World War II. Ted returned to active duty again in the Korean War from 1952 to 1953. He flew 39 combat missions in Korea and was the wingman for the future astronaut John Glenn. He was awarded the Air Medal with two Gold Stars.

Ted had many nicknames but the nickname "The Kid" was known for many years. With the prejudices in baseball at that time, if word got out that Ted's mother was Mexican-American he would have been a target to not just the fans but also players and he would have been banned from playing baseball. Ted Williams was inducted into the Baseball Hall of Fame on July 25, 1966.

Golf

Many Hispanic men and woman made a difference in the professional game of golf. At an early age, many Hispanic golfers began earning money on the golf course as caddies, by doing this they began to learn the game up close and started to see why many enjoyed golf. In time, some became the best golfers in the world and were inducted into the World Golf Hall of Fame.

Stamp issued in 1995

A few of the most well-known Latino golfers are:

Lee Trevino, a Mexican-American from Texas. He had a 40-year career playing golf. He was a member of the Professional Golf Association (PGA), and won six major championships. In the Golf Digest Magazine they named him as the fourteenth golfer of all times. In 1981, he was elected into the World Golf Hall of Fame.

Juan Antonio "Chi-Chi" Rodríguez, from Puerto Rico. In 1963, he won the Denver Open and eight more major titles on the PGA Tour, receiving the Hispanic Recognition Award in 1986. In 1992, he was the first Puerto Rican to be inducted into the World Golf Hall of Fame.

Lorena Ochoa, from Mexico. She won three majors: The Women's British Open, the Kraft Nabisco Championship in 2008, and the LPGA (Ladies Professional Golf Association). She was the leader in 2006, 2007 and 2009 golf tours. In 2003, she was LPGA Rookie of the Year. She was the second youngest LPGA player.

Camilo Villegas, from Colombia. As an amateur Latino golfer he won the Mexican Open in 2002, and a Players Amateur golf tournament in 2003, also winning the 2007 Coca-Cola Tokai Classic Japan Golf Tour. He won first place at the Colombian Open in 2001.

Nancy Lopez, a Mexican-American from California. At the age of nine, she won the California State Golf Championship for her age group. At age 12, she won the New Mexico Women's Amateur. She was the Rookie Golf Player of the Year in 1978. In 1987, she was the youngest golfer in the LPGA (Ladies Professional Golf Association) to be inducted into the Hall of Fame.

Tennis

Hispanics have had a big impact in the game of Tennis. It wasn't until the 1950s and 60s that Hispanics came into the game of tennis, and some are in the International Tennis Hall of Fame in Newport, Rhode Island.

Stamp issued in 1995

Listed below are a few of the most well-known Latino Tennis players:

Ricardo "Pancho" Alonso Gonzales, from the United States. In 1969, at the age of 41, he played the longest tennis game in history at Wimbledon. The game lasted 5 hours 12 minutes, and he won. In 1949, he won the Davis Cup. From 1952-1960, he was the World's #1 tennis player.

Francisco Olegario Segura, also known as "Pancho" or "Segoo," was a tennis player from Ecuador. He won the National Collegiate Singles Championship three years straight from 1943 to 1945, and ranked #3 in all those years. In 1944, he won the U.S. Clay Courts Championship. In 1946, he won the U.S. Indoors. In 1950 and 1952 he was the World Co-No.1. He wrote the book, *Pancho Segura's Championship Strategy: How to Play Winning Tennis.*

Beatriz "Gigi" Fernández, from Puerto Rico. She was the first Puerto Rican to win an Olympic Gold Medal with Mary Jose Fernández, and the first to be in the International Tennis Hall of Fame. As a professional, she was ranked #17. At the age of 49, she was voted 10th most influential Hispanic female athlete.

María "Mary" José Fernández, from the Dominican Republic. She won Orange Bowl junior titles in 1985. Turning professional in 1991, she won the doubles title at the Australian Open. She won a Gold Medal in women's doubles with Gigi Fernández in the 1992 Olympic Games.

Rosemary "Rosie" Casals, from the U.S. She had a reputation as a rebel in tennis. She won over 90 tournaments in two decades. In 1972, at Wimbledon she was nearly excluded for not wearing an all-white outfit. Later, she became known as the player in bright colored clothes.

Hispanic Artists for United States Stamps

Hispanic artists have been designing United States stamps as art directors and stamp designers. Hispanic artwork has a strong presence in the U.S., including stamps. The art on U.S. stamps reflect achievements in Hispanic history and culture. The artists' inspiration and expression of art and design comes from many different sources: drama, music, theater and dance. Thus, Hispanic heritage can be shared through the mail by placing these stamps on the envelopes.

Tropical Fruit

There are five different tropical fruit stamps that were issued all at the same time. Each fruit is pictured cut in half to see the inside of the fruit. They are pomegranate, kiwi, star fruit, papaya, and guava. All five stamps were done in bright colors to reflect their tasty flavors.

The artist for Tropical Fruit stamps is Sergio Baradat, a Cuban illustrator. Baradat's other stamps include *Let's Dance Mambo,* and for the United Nations Stamps he created the International Year of Forest, *Année internationale Des Forêts*, International Year of Forest, and *Internationales Jahr der Wälder* stamps, all created in 2011.

Stamps issued in 2008

Garden of Love

Stamps issued in 2011

The ten Garden of Love stamps is a way to send a loved one a very nice letter that arrives with a stamp showing love. These stamps can be placed on an envelope for Valentine's Day, Mother's Day, birthday, an anniversary or any occasion a sender wants to show affection to a loved one. On the sheet of Garden of Love stamps there are ten different stamps and they all have different symbols of love. There are bright flowers, butterflies, strawberries, and doves. The vines pictured on the ten stamps flow from one stamp to another. All the designs shown have a heart on each stamp.

The artist for the Garden of Love is José Ortega. He illustrated other stamps, *Let's Dance Salsa* and *Love with Kisses*.

Martín Ramírez

Martín Ramírez (1895-1963) was a self-taught Mexican artist. Ramírez came to California from Mexico looking for work. After the Great Depression, he was returning back home to Mexico but was detained by California police in 1931. Because he spoke only Spanish he was unable to communicate with police so he was placed in a psychiatric hospital. He spent more than 30 years there and died in the psychiatric hospital in California. While in the hospital he began drawing. After Ramírez would finish a drawing he would throw it in the trash and would begin drawing again. Many of his art pieces survived when a nurse noticed his work and began saving them. More than 40 years after his death his art was noticed.

Ramírez is known as one of the greatest self-taught artists of the 20th century. Many of his drawings are of men riding horses, religious figures, trains, the Madonna, animals and landscapes. In January 2007, the American Folk Museum in New York opened their doors for the first major retrospective exhibition of Martín Ramírez's artwork. Between 100 and 300 of his artworks are displayed across America in art galleries.

Stamps issued in 2015

Forever Hearts

These two heart-shaped stamps are in two colors, red and white. The heart is the romantic symbol of love. What better way to send a letter to a loved one than with a stamp in the shape of a heart. In the Forever Heart stamp, the word "forever" is configured in the shape of a heart.

Antonio Alcalá is the stamp designer. He served on the Postmaster General's Citizens Stamp Committee from 2010 to 2011. His artworks have won awards for National and International design for Print Communication Arts and Graphics, including the National Gallery of Arts, the Library of Congress, and the United States Holocaust Memorial Museum.

Stamps issued in 2015

Summer Harvest

Some fruits and vegetables are grown year round. The Summer Harvest stamps depict corn, tomato, cantaloupe and watermelon. All four Harvest Stamps were released at the California State Fair-Cal Expo in Sacramento, in California on July 11, 2015.

Antonio Alcalá is the art director, and the artist is Michael Doret.

Stamps issued in 2015

Quilled Paper Heart

The ancient art forms of quilling began during the Renaissance, a period from the 14th and 17th centuries. Quilling are small narrow strips of paper in different colors used to make decorative forms of art. During the Renaissance, quilling began with the French and Italians decorating bibles, book covers and ornaments. The quilling of paper can be of many different designs.

Stamp issued in 2016

This Quilled Paper Heart stamp is a heart shaped stamp made of different cuts of color paper strips and glued together to form the heart shape. Quilled Paper Heart stamps are used on envelopes during Valentine's Day, weddings, birthdays and other occasions.

The Art Director and Designer is Antonio Alcalá.

Delicioso

The *Delicioso* stamps were issued in celebration of Hispanic foods that are from Mexico, North and South America and the Caribbean. They are: *tamales, flan, sancocho, empanadas, chile relleno* and *ceviche*. All six *Delicioso* foods can be made in many variations.

Stamps issued in 2017

Tamales, a traditional Mesoamerican food made of *masa* (corn flour dough), wrapped in corn husks and steamed with different types of meats. There are also sweet *tamales*. *Tamales* date back as early as 8000 to 5000 B.C. to the Aztec and Maya civilizations.

Flan dates back to ancient Rome and Spain, it is an elegant rich dessert served for any occasion. The Latin word for *flan* is *flado* (flat cake), a sweet custard made with caramelized sugar.

Sancocho, is a traditional soup or stew from South American, consisting of large pieces of different meats or fish and vegetables with broth.

Empanadas are a pastry turnover served as an appetizer or dessert. They are tasty breads baked or fried and stuffed with various types of different fruits or meats.

Chile Relleno is a Mexican meal consisting of a chili pepper stuffed with different types of cheeses or meats, dipped in egg batter, and deep-fried or baked.

Ceviche is a Mexican and South American seafood dish dating back over 2,000 years. Ceviche is made of different types of fish mixed with lemon, onions and chili peppers.

John Parra is the artist with direction from Antonio Alcalá.

National Museum of African American History and Culture

The National Museum of African American History and Culture (NMAAHC) is the 19th Smithsonian museum, it is located at the National Mall in Washington, D.C. It has over 37,000 items in its collection with subjects in art, religion, civil rights and slavery. There were earlier attempts to establish an African-American museum in 1915. Then in 1970 interest was revived, and a big push to establish the museum began. In 1988, a special legislative committee started the authorization process for 2003, and in 2006, a site was established. The opening ceremony was held on September 24, 2016, led by U.S. President Barack Obama.

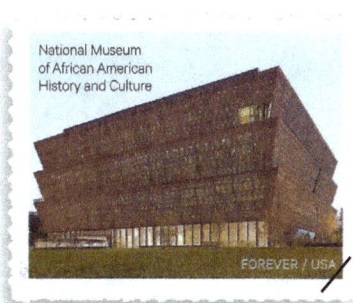

Stamps issued in 2017

Uncle Sam's Hat

The Uncle Sam's Hat stamp represents the patriotic spirit of our country. The hat colors are those of the American flag: red, white and blue. Each of the eight different shaded faces depicted on the stamp wear an Uncle Sam's hat, and they represent Americans of different ethnic and racial diversity who contributed to the building of the United States of America. The name "Uncle Sam" began after a businessman named Samuel Wilson, called Uncle Sam by his workers, began supplying beef for the United States Army during the War of 1812. Wilson's containers were stamped: "U.S. government property," and soldiers began calling it "Uncle Sam's meat." This led to the establishment of the term Uncle Sam.

Stamps issued in 2017

Art director for both stamps is Antonio Alcalá.

www.ingramcontent.com/pod-product-compliance
Lightning Source LLC
Chambersburg PA
CBHW052144110526
44591CB00012B/1852

MY DEEPEST HEART'S DEVOTIONS 3

AN AFRICAN WOMAN'S DIARY - BOOK 3

GERTRUDE KABATALEMWA

Edited by NONA BABICH AND TERESA SKINNER
Photography by ALISA ALBERS
Photography by TERESA SKINNER

ISBN: 978-1-950123-23-0

Copyright © 2019 by Teresa Skinner

Unless otherwise indicated, all Scripture quotations are taken from the Holy Bible, King James Version - Public Domain Scripture quotations marked (ESV) ® Bible (The Holy Bible, English Standard Version®), copyright © 2001 by Crossway, a publishing ministry of Good News Publishers. Used by permission. All rights reserved."

Scripture quotations marked (NIV) are taken from the Holy Bible, New International Version®, NIV®. Copyright © 1973, 1978, 1984, 2011 by Biblica, Inc.™ Used by permission of Zondervan. All rights reserved worldwide. www.zondervan.com The "NIV" and "New International Version" are trademarks registered in the United States Patent and Trademark Office by Biblica, Inc.™

All rights reserved.

No part of this book may be reproduced in any form or by any electronic or mechanical means, including information storage and retrieval systems, without written permission from the publisher, except for the use of brief quotations in a book review.